One Small Trout

By

R. E. Long

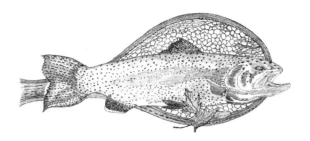

One Small Trout

Cover image:

R.E. Long

Illustrated By:

R.E. Long

Special Thanks to my friend Neil Travis for all of his insight and assistance

ISBN-13: 978-1496028884

ISBN-10: 1496028880

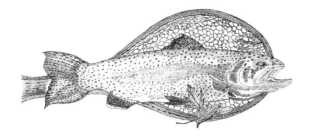

"Good luck and enjoy the water."

R.E.Long Sr.

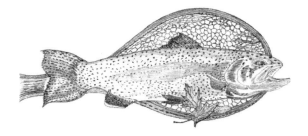

Wading Limestone

The dance of a struggling Sulfur mayfly drifted past my waders as I watched the display in anticipation. To the unaccustomed eye one would think it was merely a bug struggling in its death throes, but to the trained eye it was the emergence of life. The diminutive mayfly's wings were bent and wrinkled at first, yet beginning to unfold like the canvas of an age-old clipper ship catching its first wind as it left the Philadelphia harbor. Life's metamorphosis was beginning amid the humidity of a 90degree July day that was slowly waning. An ecosystem born of the rich 58degree limestone water was providing the hatch pursued by so many fly fishermen like myself.

R.E. Long

A child of Pennsylvania, my ancestors arrived in Philadelphia in 1734 and settled with their Pennsylvania Dutch heritage in the Red Hill area north of Conshohocken, PA. They would move North and West some, but most would never leave the limestone waters of Pennsylvania. As a result, two-hundred and forty-four years later a 7 year old boy would hook his 1st trout in the cold waters of Fishing Creek in Columbia County. From that point forward those waters would course through my veins, drawing me back again-and-again. As life and its pursuits would pull me elsewhere, I would always find time to visit. Yet a journey through Pennsylvania's storied trout waters can take more than a lifetime. There is a long heritage among their many hatches and crystal clear pools, where trout are found and fishermen are said to lose themselves. The white-lined fins of a native Brook trout in the headwaters, and the buttery gold-hued belly of a wild brown from the tail-out of a plunge-pool all hold an allure that has remained unmatched no matter where I found myself. It's the Great Blue Heron standing guard as the sentinel of these waters and the Blue-winged Teal whistling their song as they pass overhead. The cackle of a roosted gobbler in the morning dew and the call of a great horned owl announcing its evening hunt as dusk falls are like book-ends to the pages of time. From the mountain streams of central Pennsylvanian north of Interstate #80 to the spring creeks of Dutch Country, a symphony of countless waters playing over limestone and slate has defined much of my 50 years both on the water and at the tying bench.

The plethora of hatches encountered, offer the fly tyer countless opportunities to apply their skills at the bench. Though decades of modern tying have produced an unimaginable list of patterns traditionally used with success each season, I would find myself deliberating at my vise, trying variations of both design and materials on new and existing patterns. The many years have seen plenty of patterns come-and-go, yet a steady handful have remained as a reflection of my time spent. Most are specific patterns that have been time proven on particular waters, while others have been born in limestone, but fished coast-to-coast. A testament to the class of water waded and the flies they have spawned. While Pennsylvania has been the piscatorial hunting grounds of many a well-known fly fisherman, with countless books and the colorful histories of some of the most well-known waters. It is also a haven for the layman, content only to work the day with the hopes of plying their skills for an evening escape. Its rich outdoor heritage is what I grew up with, and it is that characteristic of the state that keeps its eyes on the future of these precious waters.

So it is that I found myself standing thigh-deep in one of my favorite haunts, watching the mayflies as they struggle skyward toward the haven of branches overhead. Swallows in elegant fashion swoop in for their evening meal to the dining music of Cicada's serenading their feast. Rise-forms are beginning to show as well, as if the trout had been queued to join in the orchestra. Their steady noses identifying pods of fish staged in their feeding lies across the pool, staking claim to their seats for the evening's banquet. Concentrating on a single steadily rising fish I drop my offering of thread and feather upstream of its lie and watch as my fly slips away in the swirl of a disappearing nose. The lift of my rod brings the weight of a fish to hand and I know in an instant the familiar dance as I naturally follow. The lead of which is 14 inches of stream bred brown trout....I am home.

Weeds

Stepping off the path along the road and onto the greenway trail, I picked my way along the stream while looking for a likely place to enter the water. Having gone only a short 100 yards or so, I had already had my fill of trail-crossing spider webs and mosquitos. I needed the water. Water would be my relief, both for the cooling on my legs and the cooling down of my psyche. A few more yards brought me to the edge of a small clearing where the stream S-turned through the corner of a horse pasture. Pausing to watch the water I could see a small ball of midges dancing over the head of the first pool. In a few more moments the much appreciated snout of a rising fish appeared below the dancing flies. Now came the hard part....casting to them.

The weeds were waist high to the edge of the bank, and the stream bottom was far too silty in that section to enter the water so close to the fish. It would take a long reach and a little effort to stay above the vegetation. On my first cast, with sweat running into my eyes, I placed my Griffiths gnat on the money. The drift brought a short-rise, which was followed by an inadvertent setting of the hook into nothing but air which landed my tippet in the willows slightly behind my position and to my right. AGH! $#!@!, was my instinctive response as I reeled in all of my slack and fought back through the brush to free myself. It was not a good start. After 5 minutes of struggling with willow branches and 7X tippet, I turned to find my rising fish gone. So I moved on upstream in search of another.

The stream was the type of water that whether or not it even held any fish, it was still beautiful to the eye. The mornings dew was burning off with the expected 95-degree heat that was on its way, and the only sounds to be heard over the stream were my legs pushing through the brush and this year's Cicadas. Fighting my way through some greenbrier, I looked up to see a muskrat swimming through the next hole. I stood accounting for my gear as I watched the water to no avail. No risers. The next 100 yards were tough as

One Small Trout

well. The deer trail I was on petered out quickly, and a fly rod is not greenbrier conducive. I half stumbled, half lunged out into the meadow as I exited the last of it, sweated wet and not a happy camper. However, the meadow ahead looked promising.

Edging closer to the bank without spooking anything, I gained a vantage point where I could see three nice runs in a row. And at the head of the middle pool several fish were working. Life was getting better. Applying all of the ninja skills that I don't have, I was eventually able to creep into place on a small outcropping of rock about 10 feet below the tail-out of the middle pool. It would be about a 50 foot cast, but I had nothing but stream in my back cast, or so I thought. On my last stroke forward I gave a little extra punch, and found the only stalk of reed that was 1 foot higher than everything surrounding it. Again, a low mumbling of expletives was heard. But this time I moved as slowly as possible backwards to my tippet, careful not to disturb the water. Regardless of my efforts however, the result was a new tippet. I took a breath, wiped my face off with a bandanna, and found my perch of rock once more. This time, I would remain the Heron. I refused to even look up at the rising fish, of which I could still hear greedily gulping down floating midges. I took extra time to calmly tie on another tippet and fly, and get all of my gear straight before even turning towards or thinking about a cast. They were still working. This time I looked carefully around me both in an effort to slow myself down, and to avoid a repeat performance of my last casting attempt. On my first cast the fly landed perfectly, curling to the left into the main run at the head of the pool. And just as my mind was saying "right about there", it happened. The nose came up, and within the rise form fly disappeared. The feeling of accomplishment rushed through me as if I had just felt the thump of a walk-off home run! I stood smiling as the bounce of the fish ran through my hand while I laid the rod to the side, pulling the fish into the calm of the pool. It wasn't a big fish, but the wild brown colors jumped out at me as it came to hand. Nowhere in nature is there a brighter orange than the flank-spotting of a wild brown trout. It's an attribute that never fails to catch my eye. I released the gem of a fish and watched as it somehow disappeared instantly despite the crystal clear water.

Standing, I noticed how my entire body felt relieved. The stress of the mornings briar patches, heat and line-catching weeds were gone....just like that. At first my mind wanted to share a personal fist-pump with the accomplishment of overcoming those obstacles. But as I stood there looking over the water I realized that it was not in "spite" of the weeds that I had caught that fish. It was "because" of those weeds that it had happened. At times it takes a struggle, or a little adversity to force us to slow down and pay attention to what is truly necessary. Where a perceived personal failure can cause one to focus just enough, and allow you in turn, to succeed.

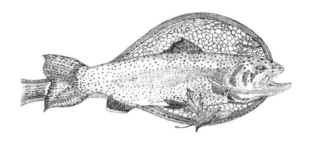

Penns Grannom

The Penns Grannom is a variation of the fluttering caddis style pattern, adapted to the streams of Pennsylvania that I frequent most. I tie the Penns Grannom in a size #14 as standard, with a hackle one size smaller than the hook. It fishes excellently dead-drift or skittered, and oftentimes seems to do better the more chewed up it becomes.

Penns Grannom Recipe

Hook: #14 1X Fine Dry

Thread: 8/0 Brown Uni-thread

Abdomen: Turkey Tail Fibers

Under-wing: Natural Dun CDC

Wing: Light Elk Hair

Thorax: Olive-Brown Orvis Spectrablend

Hackle: Brown #16 (1X Smaller)

One Small Trout

<u>Tying Instructions</u>

1- Tie in the 3-4 wild turkey tail fibers at the 1/3 point of the shank, and wrap back to the point of the barb.

2- Form a thread loop capturing the fibers in it, and spin it into a tight dubbing brush. Wrap the fibers forward to the 1/3 point of the shank and tie off.

3- Tie in a small tuft of natural dun CDC feather at the 1/3 point with the tips extended one gap length past the bend of the hook.

4- Clean, stack and tie in a small wing of elk hair, overlapping the same length as the CDC fibers. Trim the butts, overwrap and add a small drop of head cement.

5- Tie in a #16 brown hackle.

6- Dub a slight head of spectrablend.

7- Wrap the hackle forward and tie off.

8- Whip finish and head cement.

R.E. Long

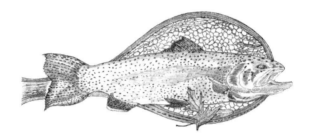

Falls Gold

Pulling my truck into the parking lot along Tulpehocken Creek in Central Pennsylvania, I found myself lacing up my boots alongside several early morning joggers. The half dozen or so fisherman you would expect to find through early fall were gone. The leaves were all off the trees, and the hatch activity could be expected to have gone along with them. We had been fortunate up until now to only have a few frosty mornings and maybe an inch of snow on a few blustery days. So with a December day beginning in the 50's, along with no rain, I chose to take a few remaining hours of vacation and fish the morning. My fall on the

21

water had come-and-gone with me in the tree stand chasing deer with bow in hand. In place of my time on the water amongst the reddening maples catching fall trout, the archery season had graced me with a close shot, straight arrow and a fat young buck. And though not much for the wall, it was perfect table-fare for friends and family through the holidays. So while not really complaining, and rightfully so, I was long overdue for some piscatorial communion. As I finished rigging, I found myself walking in silence down the wooded trail to the stream edge, just as the last of the joggers in neon-striped sports gear finished their stretching and left the parking lot in a trot.

Today I was rigged for prospecting. My 5 weight Far-and-Fine was rigged with a 5 foot thread Furled leader, looped to a 5 foot section of 5X fluorocarbon. Tied on the end was a #10 Golden Retriever pattern, and looped into the leader just above my tippet junction was a ½" thing-a-ma-bobber. I fully expected not to change this pattern throughout the morning, as it was my standard for cold weather nymphing. Moving to the head of the 1st pool above the bridge, I settled in as the familiar feel of the cold current enveloping my legs relaxed me with a sense of familiarity. It's a feeling similar to a warm pair of broken-in slippers you wear as you settle into a favorite chair in front of a fire. Bringing a sense of home, with the sound of a crackling fire replaced by the rippling sounds of water as it comes

One Small Trout

against your legs which are intruding into its current. I stripped out enough line to get a cast working, and then in what may have remotely resembled a cast, flopped my line and rig at the head of the hole...an inglorious yet effective cast none-the-less. Following the indicator with the tip of my rod I was caught slightly off-guard by a quick dip of a strike and clumsily lifted the rod to set the hook. The pulsing on the end of my line meant one thing. I had picked up my first fish of the day despite my poor efforts, and soon was admiring a 14 inch brown. It was a beautiful fish as the yellows and gold of fall color was already giving way to the winters silvery sheen. A quick flip of the tail and I was rinsing both my hands and fly in the water and looking upstream, a few casts later and I was again moving upstream to the next section of the run.

Most of the morning went as such, a good number of strikes with the stream giving up several nice brown trout. No high pressure fishing, just a nice day of prospecting to water I knew to holds trout. The temperature never warmed much above 55 degrees and there was no significant midge activity, but as with any water that you are confident holds fish, the expectation of a strike never wanes. And so it was that kept the rhythm going, trying to get as much stream in during the hours that I had. I moved into position at the head of one of the deeper stretches and was about as far upstream as I could go without leaving the water. With my first 3 casts I had nothing to speak of, except for a slight "dink" of the indicator that almost made me flinch. My 4th cast drifted through the same area and just about when I thought it had been my imagination, the indicator dipped below the surface. A quick lift of the rod was greeted with a heavy fish. A VERY heavy fish to be exact! It took about 3 pulses of the rod to make up my mind that I needed to get this fish on the reel fast or I would regret any hesitation. True to the mark just as the last of the loose coils were securely on the reel the fish shot downstream like a rocket, taking with it all of my freshly reclaimed line. I watched as the fish seemed to roll at the tail of the pool as if giving up to my palm on the reel. I just caught the glimpse of gold and the hint of a very large brown trout when I also realized that I was not breathing. Standing alone in the stream the nervous exhale came with an uncontrolled laugh of excitement. "Me and a fish", I thought to myself with another chuckle out loud. And then it turned again! The fish ran upstream faster than I could keep up with the reel and I was left stripping line in manually to keep tension. As it came even with me it paused on the bottom as if resting. The dull vibration of line tension, the fish and the stream current seemed to hum through my hand as I kept pressure on. And then, like a Pacific Salmon in a run of defiance in a glacier-colored Northwest River, it began to surge upstream in 2-3 foot runs. It worked upstream, unstoppable except when I applied pressured about 20 yards above where I stood,

One Small Trout

then with one final surge it left the water leaping 2 feet out of the water like a miniature golden tarpon and SLAPPED down hard on the surface. I was stunned....partly because of the power the fish had displayed....but also because it had just revealed itself to be a large Sucker!

And just like that, as I stood in amazement, the fight in the fish began to subside and it slowly rolled against the current as I worked him back downstream to my position. Too large to grab with one hand, I brought it sideways against my thighs in the water and pinned it to me as the tail wrapped halfway around my right leg with the current. It was easily 24" in length and a beautiful fish. Its white belly gave way to buttery-gold which blended into a dark metallic gold flank. A quick twist of the fly from the meaty lip and I held the fish out of the water for a moment with both hands. It was clearly the largest sucker I had caught on any tackle in Pennsylvania, and it pleased me to no end to have landed it. I lowered the fish back into the water and without hesitation it shot back to the pool with quite a bit of strength. I stood there in thought for a moment, realizing that though it shocked me when I realized the type of fish it was, I never once felt the inevitable let-down that is normal whenever you realize you've hooked a sucker in trout waters. This fish fought as well as any I had ever hooked and was the first and only fish I had put on the reel all year. Looking upward I touched the tip of my nose in acknowledgement and understanding. A small piece of Falls Gold had been saved and offered up. It's amazing, I thought to myself with a smile, that even when you are certain of what it is you want and seek; sometimes the pieces of treasure you receive and need the most are so different....and completely unexpected?

Gifts

This past Father's Day, I was treated to a number of gifts and thoughts that truly made the day a special one. From BBQ essentials and a wonderful family display, to a picnic breakfast in the park and gift cards to places that sell fly fishing gear. I was a truly blessed father. A fact that didn't come as a shock, since I already knew that. My youngest son then proposed the main part of his gift, which was to declare the schedule as well. I was to be treated to breakfast, and then I would be taking him fly fishing. "But we have to go where we can get in the water", was his stipulation. Meaning, we needed to be fishing a stream for trout. I smiled and agreed, knowing full well the implication was that I would be the guide/ untangler/ net guy for the day. A task in itself that isn't all bad however, and I accepted with a smile.

Having a couple lawn casting sessions and one day last summer on the water, he is in the beginning stages of grasping the art of fly fishing. However, I do find that whenever it is something in which he himself chooses to pursue, the learning curve is fairly short. And at just short of 11yrs old any desire to pursue and enjoy the outdoors is encouraged on my behalf. The drive would be two hours which brought a few moans of realization, but in the end he was all-in. My concern was the heat and the later start. It's always a good thing with youngsters to stack the odds in their favor since no fish and boredom can kill an outdoor experience for them in a second, sending them running for their electronics as fast as the jingle of an ice-cream truck on a hot summer day sends them running for the curb. So feeling the pressure I tried to pick the most likely spot, with easy access and the likelihood of fish. The decision was for a place in Pennsylvania near my hometown, where I actually fished with my Dad when I was at about that same age.

Pulling in, Mom sat on the bank with a chair and some reading material, and we began the process of rigging up. Things were looking promising as his attention and questions increased. Moving to the water his shuffling feet gave away his impatience as I quickly

One Small Trout

went through a lesson on casting and using the water tension to help with the nymph/indicator rig he would be using. I finally handed him the rod after at least three "I knows" to each of my points. And he promptly made his best effort to fatally birds-nest a braided leader and tippet, which prompted another round of shuffling impatient feet as I worked the problem out; all the while worrying the delay would kill the drive. But he hung in there quite well. I made one quick demonstration before handing him the rod, and to my surprise I hooked a small creek chub in the process. This lit a fire even hotter under him and he quickly demanded that he was "good" and to give him the rod. I watched him, with no small bit of humor, as I observed all of the stubbornness I was born with standing there before me, contained in a miniature 14 year old package.

He began to catch on fairly quick to the process of roll casting and tension casting with the heavier nymph rig, and soon he was taking steps upstream and looking across the water for his next targets. He worked his way through the shallow sunlit water with no takes, which did not surprise me at all. I pointed toward a small run next to the bridge abutment upstream of us and tried to guide him in that direction; figuring that a slight nudge would make him feel the decision was more this than mine. It worked nicely and in short order we were closing in on the likely spot. His casting was improving with each attempt. I asked for the rod twice to give him an example of how to get his rig in the right place to manage a few odd currents, and to my surprise he willingly gave up the rod and paid attention. The realization of this fact caught me off guard as he took the rod and duplicated my efforts exactly. Several times he asked for my hand to get him over some slick spots where his rubber soled hip boots were giving way. At least he wasn't too stubborn to ask for help when it involved the possibility of getting wet, I thought with a chuckle.

We moved into position for the pool under the bridge and I asked for the rod one more time, showing him how this particular current would need to be fished. He took the rod and moved to where I stood as I backed away, and on the second cast watched the indicator disappear. I quickly instructed him to take up his slack and lift the rod, resulting in a bouncing 9 inch trout as it began its dance of defiance to the hook which it had so rudely just encountered. I was hoping it would remain in the safety of the deep plunge pool, and, as luck would have it, it cooperated. He was fighting the fish out loud as everything that crossed his mind during the event came out in spoken form. And as I slid the net under it, he celebrated with a fist pump and a "YES!" He was in the moment, and we shared smiles and congratulations. On top of it being his first trout on a fly rod, it was also the completion of his "trout slam", since he had previously taken a brookie and a brown. His goal

One Small Trout

of catching all three had been attained. We fished the hole for another 20 minutes and he was able to roll one more even larger rainbow, but failed to hook-up. As we turned to walk back towards the car and his Mom, he commented, "We're not done are we Dad?"

"Absolutely not" I answered.

"Good!" was his reply, as he made his way across the slick rocks and up the bank like a pro, without even a second thought about needing my hand.

Watching him walk from behind with the rod in his hand I realized that the intended gift was not the most important one achieved on this Father's Day. What I had been given was worth so much more than a chance to spend time on the water. We would both forever carry these memories on our journeys downstream even when I am no longer at his side. And though now gone from our midst, I am certain my Dad was smiling down upon his grandson on this day.

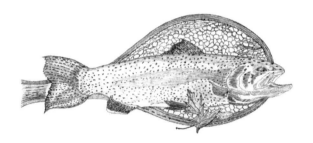

Copper Jake

The Copper Jake was originally named by the turkey tail feathers from a Jake I had just taken. It is one of my favorite searching patterns and has brought fish to hand on nearly every piece of water I have fished. I also tie this pattern with a black tungsten bead-head. Both varieties do extremely well.

Copper Jake Recipe

Hook: #14 Orvis Beadhead hook

Thread: 6/0 Dark Brown Uni-thread

Tail: Moose body hair

Abdomen: Brown Squirrel

Rib: Copper wire

Wingcase: Turkey Tail fibers

Flashback: Pearl Flashabou

Thorax: Brown Squirrel

One Small Trout

Tying Instructions

1- Start thread, move to the bend of the hook and tie in the moose body hair tail.

2- Move the thread back to the eye of the hook and tie in the copper wire, Pearl Crystal flashabou and the turkey tail, in that order.

3- At the rear of the shank and dub a slender tapered abdomen.

4- Pull the turkey tail fiber wingcase forward over the abdomen and tie off.

5- Pull the flashabou forward and tie off.

6- Wrap the ribbing forward, tie of and clip at the end of the abdomen.

7- Pull the turkey tail and flashabou back out of the way and dub a substantial thorax.

8- Pull the turkey tail fibers forward and tie off and then follow with the flashabou and whip finish.

9- Coat the thorax portion of the wingcase with head cement/epoxy/goo of choice. Whip finish.

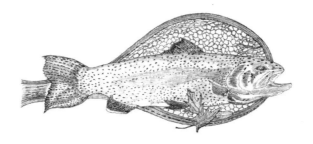

Lake Somewhere

Turning right at the intersection my buddy quickly pointed to the curb on the right, "Right there! Jump up right there and park in the grass!" I obeyed, leaving my turn signal on and slowing down as 2 different people behind me made use of their horns. I waved apologetically to them in the rear-view mirror, knowing they could not possibly understand why I was suddenly slowing down to jump the curb in this particular spot.

Pulling the Xterra to a quick stop I laughed. "Where's the lake?"

My buddy laughed and pointed out his window at the tall vegetation, "Just on the other side of these" he said smiling.

I laughed out loud as we climbed out of the vehicle and turned to the back of the car. Looking around we were just off the road and over the curb, not more than 50 feet from a major 4-way intersection. It was 6pm and at the moment all four lanes were full. As we donned our waders I could see the looks on those rush-hour faces, as they turned unknowingly while sitting at the light only to see what? Two weird looking fella's in tan waders rigging up fly rods. One spectator mouthed clear-as-day out his window "What the hell?" as he looked me straight in the eyes. I smiled back at him like I was holding a big secret. He rolled down the window just as the light turned green and while laughing yelled out "GOOD LUCK!" I waved back and laughed myself. Since I too was a little caught off guard and really had no idea what to expect.

"You're going to be wading in a mud bottom through lily pads, so take it slow." He said, snapping me back into the moment. "And they are not leader shy so rig accordingly." He added. Tying on a black deer hair diving popper I gave a nod of acknowledgement in response to his guidance. "The place is full of 12" to 18" bass, slab bluegills and the occasional large pike," He added.

One Small Trout

"Pike?" I said suddenly looking up. "Ok then". He had promised me a honey hole in a place that I would never suspect.....and so far he was right on track.

With rods rigged we stepped down through the wall of reeds and cattails. I wish I could say that the sounds of the intersection melted away in the background. But I can't. I try to save all of my really good lying for real fish stories. So while it did get a little subdued, its presence never left us throughout the evening. As we stepped through the lake came into view. It was perfect! In front of us was about 6 acres of lake which was two thirds covered with lily pads. As I stood looking out, the rings of rise-forms and large fish swirling were everywhere! He gave me the lay of the land as far as where we would be able to wade, then gave me the near bank and he walked around to fish one of the lily shallows. Stepping down into the mid-thigh deep water, I instantly sunk to my waist. He was right, it would be slow going. On my second cast I had a large bass swirl my popper, but all I managed to do was lip it. Moments later, a 'whoop" from across the lake made me turn to see my buddy with a bass in hand. Well, I thought to myself, he was right. Over the course of the next 2 hours I was able to miss a good number of bass, broke a nice fish of in the lily pad stalks and land one nice bass and a handful of bluegills. But as the sun dipped below the western tree line I began to notice the tell-tale rings of larger bluegills coming to life amongst the pads.

Knowing the bass would probably pick up as well, I clipped off the larger deer hair bug. My heart picked up a few beats as I sifted through my box and watched big swirls and Damsel flies begin their dance. I was now in my zone. I heard another "whoop" and looked up to see my buddy playing what appeared to be a nice Pike. But I was on a mission. Tying on a #10 Foam-Butt Caddis in black and grey I turned towards those rings. Not wanting the groups of chasing fish near the edges, I looked for the lone swirls in the small openings deeper in the lilies. My reward was one fat slab of a bluegill after another. The little 5wt danced and I smiled larger with every fish. At one point, I paused to get a picture of a beautiful Copper-breasted male, admiring his heft and inch thick back. It was a prime example of a nice gill and a perfect ending to my night.

Climbing out of the mud and up the bank to the truck, the pace had not slowed down since pulling in. All 4 lanes in every direction were still humming along with folks oblivious to the fishing taking place, just as I had been having passed this place many times over the years. Walking up to the truck my buddy wore a smile that was all-knowing. "Nice water isn't it?" he remarked, more as a statement than a question. My smile said it all.

One Small Trout

We had just spent 3 hours in the middle of chaos, smack in the middle a major area in South Jersey. We had fished for 3 hours and caught some very nice fish, and never saw another soul even near the water.

"What's this place called?" I asked more off-hand than anything.

He shrugged and just looked at me. "I've been fishing this lake for 10 years and have no idea. "Call it Lake Somewhere."

I agreed. "That works!" I replied. Maybe it was best that way, since once water has a given name, folks want to find out where it is. And it seems a much nicer place to fish when everybody else is driving past, wondering what those crazy guys are doing in chest waders in the middle of nowhere.

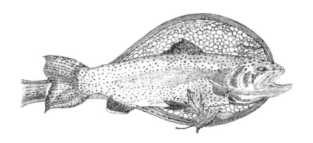

Moments in Time

The first bug left the water and took off like a lumbering Huey as it bounced and rotated upwards toward the awaiting safe haven of branches. The yellow glow of the fading light gave a brilliant contrast to the mahogany body as it appeared the sanctuary of the trees was in reach. But obviously I was not the only thing in the ecosystem that was admiring the big mayfly as a swallow suddenly hit it with an agility only nature can provide, ending the small bugs flight and hopes of procreation. I stood there contemplating what had just happened, and in that short span of time the air became filled with swallows that were in turn chasing more rising mayflies. The hatch was on.

Quickly turned to my tippet I swapped patterns to match the current activity, knowing there would be no time to lose in the brief moments ahead. The hatch did not let me down as fish slammed my fly with gusto on nearly every cast over the course of the next 30 minutes. Fish that I knew to be in the pool but had not seen sign of all day suddenly materialized to join in the frenzy. It was fly fishing nirvana for a span of time in my trout seeking life....and then it was gone. The 16 inch Cutthroat slipped from my hand with a tail-slap of gratitude and I was suddenly aware that the swallows were gone. Looking up across the pool, the rings of rising fish were gone as well. Yet the feeling of exhilaration was still there, along with a memory that would be tucked away unknowingly in my piscatorial memory bank to be relived countless times.

That evening on the Lewis River in Western Washington between the upper falls and Swift Reservoir, remains in my mind to this day even after 20-plus years of chasing fish from one coast to the other since then. Something in my mind, or about that day, I chose to save as a special nugget of gold-plated memory. It's not alone in there mind you. There are others from countless waters and amazing hatches. Some include large fish, yet others are as simple and

One Small Trout

uneventful as could be imagined. All of which, for some reason, have been retained above the remaining countless hours spent on the water. I have often thought back on why exactly that hatch was chosen? What triggered the permanent burn onto my mental hard drive? Putting my finger on the reason has remained elusive however, which at times haunts me though it should just be accepted and remembered for what it was. Oddly enough I fished that entire stretch of water dozens of times since that hatch, yet never saw that mayfly ever again. To the best of my knowledge it was a mahogany dun. But that is purely guess work since I'm pulling from memory and pictures only. I never really paused long enough to examine the fly. At the time I pulled a like-sized dark bodied haystack pattern from my box and began catching fish. Maybe it was the fact that it went so perfect. From the realization of the first sighted bug to the end of the hatch everything went 100% perfectly. In fact, I would be lying if I tried to guess just how many fish I caught in that 30 minutes. It would be more than 10, and some were well over 16 inches but beyond that I do not remember. I guess in the grand scheme of things it doesn't really matter.

It seems odd when we try to apply our own "values-at-a-glance" to our time on the water, quite often we fall short in what really matters. Since only time will tell us what was really important, it is all speculation until we wade back from downstream in life. Surprisingly to us, our minds fail to even twinkle at the memory of a big hook-nosed brown we caught back in 2005 along some spectacular water, yet we stand in awe when a particular sunset, rise of a trout, or stream setting causes us to glaze over about a day when you remember catching a single beautifully spotted fish on some non-descript creek. Or when your child, catching a fish, puts you right back to the smell of a jar of salmon eggs and your own father's voice carried on the sounds of rushing water. Your subconscious knows what matters, even when your mind in the present does not. I doubt that we are supposed to know. It is for us to live our lives on the water in hopes that at some point along the way we can understand what it all means, and what it is that we will need downstream.

So it is now....as I stand in the water under an overcast golden fall sunset. The swallows are swooping overhead and what looks like a Slate Drake hatch is coming off. My mind has already begun working in the present, telling my hands to tie on a size 12 Slate Drake Haystack. Yet as the wonderfully cold waters of the Pennsylvania mountain stream swirls around my waders I am no longer there. I am transported back to the shadows of Mt St. Helens on the Lewis River....and another obviously special moment in time.

<u>Long Cress</u>

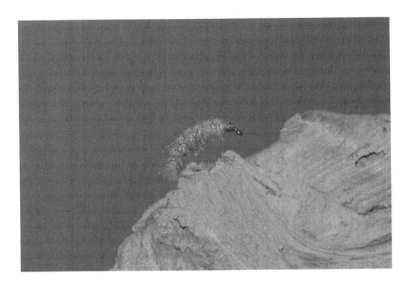

    This Cress Bug pattern was originally tied for the Yellow Breeches spring creek, yet has done well enough to become the staple Cress/scud pattern in my box over the years. It is a very simple pattern to tie, and one that I find myself needing to replenish each spring above most others.

Long Cress Recipe

Hook: #16-18 Scud or Caddis hook

Thread: 8/0 Olive Uni-thread

Abdomen: Olive Haretron

Underbody: Medium lead wire or lead substitute

Shellback: Tan CDC fibers

Rib: Fine gold wire

One Small Trout

Tying Instructions

1- Tie in your thread and build even thread base. Wrap 8-10 wraps of wire at the midpoint of the shank and overwrap well with thread to secure.

2- Move your thread back to the head and tie in your wire, wrapping back to the point even with the line of the barb of the hook.

3- Tie in your CDC fibers leaving about 1/8" of tail extended out.

4- Dub a body which slightly tapers from the tail to the mid-point, and then tapers slightly back down to the head.

5- Pull the CDC shellback forward and tie off.

6- Evenly wrap the wire ribbing forward and tie off.

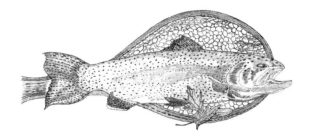

Creek Chubs

While I'm usually not often one that will speak for the whole, I feel pretty comfortable in saying that creek chubs, are for the most part the scourge of trout fishermen. On the left-hand coast, the whitefish is a close second, but on the right-hand coast the diminutive wart-headed creek chub wins when it comes to the disdain of trout fishermen. They are to the trout fishermen, what juvenile schools of sunfish are to bass fishermen. Never seeming to show themselves when expected, more often than not they choose to announce themselves whenever expectations are high and a fat wild brown is on the mind. So it was that I found myself on stream near my home.

R.E. Long

With time to fish a scarcity of late, I hit the road on a Sunday morning with expectations of trout and much needed therapeutic waters. Waders and moving water is to me the Sigmond Freud of a healthy life. They heal, calm & otherwise keep me out of trouble in more ways than one could ever put into words. So was my state of mind on this morning, and a calm period of piscatorial solitude was much needed. Pulling in to the small parking area just off the creek, I was pleasantly surprised by the lack of trucks. I was winning all the way around at this point and spirits were high as I rigged my rod and pulled on my waders. Today would be good. Walking down the bank to the first large run, I tied on a small size-16 Elk hair Caddis pattern and positioned myself to fish the majority of the run. My first cast lit exactly where I wanted it and was met with a quick swirl and short strike which I cleanly missed. Telling myself that would not happen on the next cast however, I was ready. This time the fly hit the water, travelled a scant 12 inches, and was again engulfed in a swirl. The result of my anticipation was a reflex action that would have certainly shocked the meaty lip of a 20lb carp. The little 4-weight rod snapped to attention with a quickness seldom seen on my part. I recall watching in amazement as the fly left the water, arching up-and-back towards the trees behind me, but it was also attached to the lip of a 6" creek chub! My second reaction was to keep my line out of the trees, causing me to reverse my previous reflex action. It worked.

One Small Trout

Unfortunately for the chub, it worked all too well. The fly came back to the water, and the diminutive fish kept travelling into the briars behind. For a short moment I stood looking back into the woods behind me. Was I debating going back in there to rescue the fish? No....not really. All I was doing was coming to grips with the past 4 seconds of my life, and thinking that it sure was a bad day to be a creek chub. Now I know that Izaak Walton would certainly have a few stout words on my behalf, had he been present. But he was not. A fact that again was good for me, yet bad for the creek chub.

Gathering my senses I turned back towards the water. However, the creek chub Gods were not on my side on this day, as cast after cast resulted in more chubs. After about 20 fish, I was debating whether or not the more prudent thing to do would be to leave the pool or go find that damned chub and give it a proper burial to make amends? I chose to work my way down to faster water. Maybe the warmth of the run was the problem? My decision did improve things a bit, but not in the manner intended. What I found in the faster riffles were larger chubs! Their stature was now in the 8" range. Large enough to hammer a nymph like a trout, but still, not a trout. Each fish was beginning to wear on me just a tad as I felt my therapeutic tonic of the trout stream slipping into oblivion.

R.E. Long

The sun was beginning to warm, and so was my blood pressure as I eased downstream to the next pool. My first cast was with a Caddis/Hares Ear dropper rig, and halfway through the drift my indicator fly went under. Setting the hook I was immediately treated to a nice heavy fish. "Finally!" I said out loud, just happy to set the hook on a trout. Then....I saw it. It was nearly 12" in length and fighting heartily. But it was again, a chub! Amazed, I landed the fish and looked it over. A strong cold fish, sort of attractive if you were to remove the head warts it wore. I released it with a chuckle and instantly caught 2 more just like him on the next 2 casts. They had won. If I had wanted larger fish, well then I had found them. If I had wanted a better fight, well then I had found that too. Somewhere along the line I was simply fly fishing. Somewhere along the course of the morning I went from being irritated, to catching fish. Somewhere along the line I stopped being the wart-headed individual on the "other" end of the line and began appreciating what the day had provided. In the end I was able to leave the water better off, and despite my best efforts, Creek Chubs were no longer the enemy.

Other Waters

The trip was to fish a much anticipated handful of private waters in Virginia. With plans to arrive on a Friday afternoon and hopes of two good mornings of fishing with a local guide, we had also identified a small section of public brook trout water to target Saturday evening. We figured the evening would be better spent on the water rather than in a hotel room.

Luck, and the trout gods were on our side Saturday and a morning's worth of memories were created, followed by a short shore-lunch. We then tossed our gear back in the trucks and headed for the mountains and some small stream brook trout. The guides confirmed our choice of planned water with a thumbs-up approval, and off we went. The trek was not without its issues however, since GPS and Rand McNally had a bit of dispute over just where the roads went once the blacktop stopped. But we finally found it, and in short order had our rods rigged and turned towards the big pines of the national forest. We approached the water through the humid southern summer timber and the sounds of the stream grew tantalizingly louder with each step. Then with one last push through a bit of bramble, there it was. It was a beautiful 20 foot wide, high gradient, S-curved perfection that tumbled along towards the valley below. We split up in two's, with myself and a buddy going upstream. I took high-man and turned to walk the bank upstream for the high starting point, at which point we would both be working towards each other. The entire walk was just one perfect hole after another. Arriving at a point where the stream forked I decided to begin my decent downstream. There was a perfect plunge pool at the confluence of the 2 branches and I positioned myself in knee deep water below it. I had tied on a #16 Limestone pattern, which is a merger of a stimulator and a Birds Stone pattern tied with light elk. The results? Before I even shifted weight on my boots, I had landed 3 nine-inch vermillion painted native brookies with 3 consecutive casts. My 3-weight glass rod proved to be

One Small Trout

the perfect match for the water, as fish after fish slashed and ripped the small offering of elk hair.

Moving downstream I found each hole to be almost exactly the same, providing 2 or 3 hungry brookies ready to do battle over my fly. There wasn't a soul in sight on the stream for the duration of the evening as I worked downstream. Then as the humidity had foretold, the rumblings of an evening humidity storm sounded its approach. I had just decided to pull in my line as my buddy rounded the turn below me. The smile and shaking of his head in disbelief told me everything even before he got within ear-shot. He had experienced much the same as I had and never even made it more than 3-4 pools upstream before the sounds of the approaching storm forced made him move along in search of me. We made our way back towards the truck but came up just short of beating the storm as the rain dumped hard about 100yrds short. The southern rain did itself justice, soaking us to the skin in minutes as we attempted to get out of our waders. As we sat in the car waiting on the remaining 2 guys, we looked at the map and acknowledged that we had really only fished a small portion of the 15 miles of stream in which we had just tried, both agreeing that more time would be needed to further explore the rest of the stream. The next morning found us again on more great water as drift after drift pulled up some magnificent managed trout, with each fish surpassing the 16" mark and some heading into the mid-twenties. It was a joy to experience and we made plans to come back in the very near future.

I recently got a call from that fishing partner and we turned towards discussing our previous Virginia trip. The intent of the conversation was to re-visit the private waters again. After an hour of planning over the phone, I paused and told him that what I really wanted to do down there, was spend more time on that brook trout water. The other end of the phone went silent, and I thought for sure he was a bit disappointed, wanting to catch some more of those impressive fish. But after a few moments he responded with a "Thank God!" Asking what he meant, he revealed that ever since the last trip, the brook trout water had virtually haunted him with a need to get back down there. Having felt the exact same way, we decided to head back down, but not in search of big managed fish. Rather, we would be going unguided and exploring the entire length of the other water we had visited.

Sitting at my vise a few days ago, I began to think about that phone conversation. It seemed to me to be a shining example of why it is that I have truly embraced fly fishing so strongly over the years. It's the fact that the entire experience is so much larger than any one fish. Or even any full weekend of large private water fish for that matter. What pulls me in is that moment

One Small Trout

when the air is nearly sucked out of your lungs with the first glimpse of a particular water. It's in the solitude of standing alone in water and all that encompasses the places in which trout haunt. Or the appreciation of the brilliant red flank markings shadowed in pale blue, surrounded by a vermillion pattern that only nature itself could create. It all adds up to so much more than any high-dollar gear, guided venture or all the marketing hype in the world could provide. More often than not, where I gather the purest sense of personal gratification throughout my fly fishing meanderings is in the natural perfection found in those other waters.

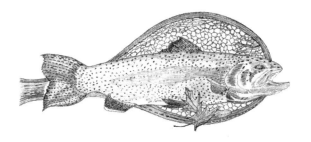

<u>Limestone</u>

The Limestone is a variation of my Satsop Stone, which was originally tied for the western salmon fly hatches. This is a scaled down and color appropriate pattern for the Northeast waters while still utilizing the attributes that have made the Satsop Stone so effective. This is my fly of choice when fishing pocket water or heavy water. It floats like a cork and always lands on its feet.

Limestone Recipe

Hook: #12 Curved Dry

Thread: 8/0 Brown Uni-thread

Tail: Light Elk Hair

Rib: Furnace hackle clipped

Abdomen: Ginger Hareline

Wing: Light Elk Hair

Thorax: Ginger Hairline

Antennae: Furnace Hackle Quills

Hackle: Cree (V-clipped on bottom)

One Small Trout

Tying Instructions

1- Clean and stack a small clump of elk hair, tie in the tail approximately gap-width in length.

2- Tie in a furnace hackle tip-first at the point of the tail

3- Dub a slender abdomen to a point slightly forward of the half-way point of the shank.

4- Wrap your furnace hackle evenly forward, tie off, and then clip it down so that only the dark center of the hackle is remaining.

5- Clean and stack a clump of elk hair and tie in the wing in Stimulator fashion. Extending the tips even with the tail.

6- Tie in both antennae, trimming them approximately twice the width of the hook gap in length.

7- Tie in your hackle, Dub a slightly tapered thorax forward. Palmer your hackle forward evenly and whip finish.

8- "V-Notch" the bottom of the hackle about half the way to the shank of the hook in depth. Position the antennae and head cement

R.E. Long

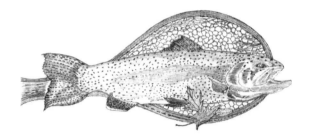

The Rise of Steel

The broadleaf ferns held water like a fresh new kitchen sponge as I squeezed my way down a narrow elk trail in search of the sounds of running water up ahead. I was only 100 yards off the trails end where I had parked my truck, and already I was soaked through from armpit to mid-thigh. 'Should have worn my waders", I thought as I glanced down at the water beaded and running down my hip-boots. But I knew that it was forecast to be in the mid 70's by noon, so waders would not have been the way to go in the long haul. It was a cool 50 degrees and a bluebird day for late September on the Olympic peninsula. Today I was on the hunt for the headwaters of the East fork of the Satsop River, in search of Sea-run Cutthroat. I had taken a fat blacktail doe with my bow earlier in the week, so with my archery tag filled the rest of the fall would be spent carrying the 7 feet of glass rod now held in my hand. And although the vast majority of my fishing is catch-and-release, sea-run cuts are my favorite eating fish. So with hopes of an evening meal of trout, I was stalking my favorite fall waters with a newly minted 3wt glass rod. With the Upper Satsop being only 8-to-12ft wide and mostly pocket water, the rod would be perfect for side-arming casts around rainforest vegetation.

As I approached the stream, the ferns gave way to the moss covered raised roots of the surrounding Fir trees and the smell of the mulch-like black soil beneath the moss was strong.. Everything seems accentuated once you get near water within the rainforest. The smell of elk was strong as I stepped out into an opening, and I glanced over just in time to see the rump of an elk slowly step off into the ferns on the far side of the stream and disappear. I stood for a moment listening to the herd slowly move off downstream, seemingly unimpressed by my existence. Yet even as the sound of their movement faded into the background noise of the stream, the strong scent of their passing hung heavily in the air. The stream edge was a jump down from the high-water mark and I tried to keep things quiet as I made my way down to the gravel. Pausing to rig up and look over the first pool upstream, I tied on a size #12 Satsop Stone pattern and put myself into position to fish

One Small Trout

the entire pool without moving. On my third cast my fly was slammed with gusto by a hungry wild fish and moment later I was dropping a 14" cutthroat into my creel. A great start, now just find that fish's twin and I would have the dinner I was looking for.

Moving up to the larger pool above me, I paused to dry and dress my fly when I noticed something in the water near the head of the run. The water was clear and only about 3ft deep in the middle of the run. There it was again. A large fish came up from the bottom like it was inspecting something floating by, and then sunk back down to the bottom. It was a BIG fish. Not being able to cast standing due to overhead vegetation, I eased down to my knees in the water where I stood bringing the cool Olympic water up over my knees where it swirled around my creel that hung in the water at my hip. While keeping my rod low at about a side-arm position I hook-cast the pattern to the head of the pool. I could see the shadow of the fish but it didn't move as my fly approached. When the current began to take my fly off of its intended drift, I began to lift my line which added a bit of unintentional drag to the fly as it swung below the fish. It was at that very moment the big fish surged and came to the top, take the fly and rolling in a boil on the surface. I lifted my rod to set the hook and my world exploded. A mere ten feet in front of me and at nearly eye level as I knelt there in the water, a 3 foot long fish exploded out of the water! Not one...not two...but 3 times in a row! Each time leaving the water while twisting in mid-air and "slapping" down hard on the surface. After the 3rd jump my mind caught up with the moment and I realized that this was not a larger sea-run cutt. I knew at that moment that it was a steelhead. And I also knew that the steady pull of an anchored fish holding the bottom in front of me now was only there out of sheer luck, since I had done literally noting after the hook-set to either retain or lose that fish. I just knelt there wide-eyed throughout, along for the ride in all of its shock and amazement.

After a few moments of applying back-and-forth side pressure, the headshakes began and he came back to the surface. This time the tactic was a steady rolling boil in the middle of the pool. Hanging on for dear life, it took two more similar runs before he finally began to tire. Then suddenly I was holding my rod high as the large fish drifted in the current downstream to my knees where I was able to tail it at last. Lifting the fish from the water, it was beautiful. Obviously having been in the river for quite a while, it had taken on the dark smoky colors of a classic rainbow. Gone were the silvers and chromes of the sea. He was a wild fish with perfect fins all around. I took a moment to measure it on my rod, which later proved it to be about 34" in length, and then focused for a bit on reviving the fish before it kicked smoothly from my hand taking station once again. I stood and gathered myself and moving slowly

One Small Trout

up the pool on the gravel to find that he was the only one. An odd lone holdover from the wild summer run, and a true gift that I had been privileged to enjoy. Taking several more nice fish through the day, I was able to creel another fat Cutthroat in the 14" range and left the stream with far more than that which I had arrived with.

Now...sitting at my tying bench 21 years later with that same little Lamiglass Firecane rod across my lap, it all comes back as if it had just happened this morning. I can once again smell the passing of the elk, feel the cold clear water on my legs and see that fish turn and rise towards my fly.

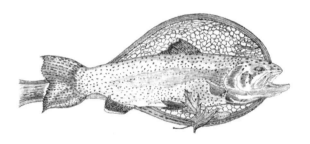

A Good Day

The morning couldn't have been better. I had six inches of silent powder that had fallen overnight to stalk through, and the morning was offering up a hint of what warmth "could" feel like as the sun glowed through the overcast sky that was still offering up a light flurry. It was Muzzle-loader season, and my hands were enjoying the warmth of the Hawken rifle's hand-rubbed walnut stock cradled in the crook of my arm. I was easing along behind five sets of fresh deer tracks, expecting to catch a glimpse of them at any moment. My hunt today was strictly for holiday jerky, with only a doe license in my possession. With no wind, mild temperatures, tracking snow and fresh tracks....Things felt good.

R.E. Long

Easing through some sparse mountain laurel, I could begin to hear the sound of the stream I knew was growing close. The tracks had begun to disperse a bit just before the laurels, and with hemlock up ahead bordering the stream it told me they were stopping to fed along the stream. Pausing to listen, my thumb found the hammer of the reproduction rifle with a re-assuring thump. It would be soon. Slipping forward a step at a time the hemlock flat came into view and I stopped in mid-step, cautious not to jerk my leg or stop to sudden, as 50 yards ahead of me they stood. To my right fed an average doe with 2 yearlings, while directly to my front stood a large old doe and a 1-to-2 year old doe quartering away feeding along the creeks edge. The rifle came up slowly as my front sight post settled on it' mark. An instant later the sound, smoke and scattering of deer was over and the old doe was down and still. She lay on the crest of the high-water -mark as I knelt next to her, slipped a sprig of laurel into her mouth and gave thanks for the gift.

Taking a seat in the snow next to her, I reflected on the hunt and took some time to rest a bit before dressing her out and beginning my drag to the truck. My initial thoughts had come to fruition. It had indeed felt like a good morning. Glancing upstream at the glass-like run to my left, I found myself staring at a rise-form. As I watched on, there were several more trout feeding as the small flakes settled straight down on the water.

One Small Trout

With the overcast sun and no wind, I had a beautiful view to watch the hatch. I could not see the trout on the bottom, but once they were a foot or so from the surface they would come into view in perfect clarity for an amazing display of feeding. They all appeared to be browns of about 10 inches, and they were feeding on a dark tannish-dun midge in the 22-24# size range. Each time, they would let the floating midge pass them by, then rise to the surface in trail to take the insect from behind. They were hunting! I wondered what their view from below was like with the windless glass surface and light flakes settling on the water? I got the sense they were experiencing the same feeling that I had so recently felt, as everything had been coming into play so perfectly when the tracks had exited the laurels. Did they "just know" that with conditions so perfect that a hatch was certain to show up? I watched them feed for quite some time, completely still and in awe of what was on display. I had not seen a rise for about 5 minutes when I realized that in my concentration the snow had dusted me white from head-to-toe.

Standing and dusting myself off, dressing the doe was quick and easy and before I knew it I was done and she was tied to the dragging rope. As I turned to make towards the truck which was about 400yds away, I looked up to see a Great Horned Owl sitting on a branch about 30 feet up and off to my left. I looked back at the remains in the snow and back up to the owl who had most likely been there watching the entire time. "It's going to be a good day isn't it?" I said out loud more as a statement than a question. The owl simply canted his head slightly and hunched its shoulders, but remained on the branch despite the sound of my voice. I guess he agreed.

Skittle

A "guide fly" is generally referred to as a simple to tie and reproduce durable pattern that catches fish pretty much everywhere. If I were a guide, the Skittle would be my "guide fly". It has caught fish for me anywhere I have asked it to, and likewise for friends and acquaintances coast –to-coast. I tie it in chartreuse, red, yellow & orange, but chartreuse has been the most consistent. I will often fish it in tandem with other colors as well when prospecting new water. Just find the flavor skittle they want.

Skittle Recipe

Hook: #12-14 Scud/Caddis hook

Thread: 6/0 Olive Uni-thread

Abdomen: 2-3 strands of Peacock Herl

Rib: Small Fluorescent Chartreuse Ultra-wire

Hackle: Brown 2X Smaller than hook size

One Small Trout

Tying Instructions

1- Tie in thread and build a good base, securing the bead in place.

2- Move the thread to the bead and tie in the wire and the peacock herl, in that order. Wrap back to the point even with the line of the barb of the hook.

3- Tie in your hackle "tip first", and sweep the fibers out from the quill.

4- Pull all 3 materials together and grab with your hackle pliers, then spin them into a tight dubbing rope. The materials will work themselves out on their own.

5- Wind evenly to the bead, tie off and whip finish.

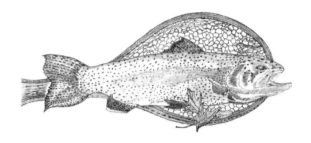

A Season for Tying

For many of us fly fishing is a year 'round
passion that we either embrace fully, or try to corral to
fit within our busy schedules. For others, it's strictly a
Spring/Summer ordeal where hatches and dry flies are
the driving emphasis for their time on the water. Once
the frosts arrive, they roll up shop and move indoors or
onto other pursuits. I personally have always carried
my time on the water into the winter months, but
admittedly mainly on selective days where Indian
summers and January thaws are welcome anomalies.
There are the normal lulls in my time on the water
caused by a few other conditions that course threw my
veins each year, that seem to overcome my fly fishing
and fly tying efforts. They come in the form of Spring
Gobblers waking me up at first light, and the velvet

bucks of early fall which prompt my bow to come off the pegs.

Yet through the year they all blend together. While chasing strutting gobbler each spring, I am scouting for antler drops and the tell-tale signs of the previous year's rut. I'm walking streams and watching for clearing waters and mid-day hatches to begin. In the fall, I am walking the furthest waters with bow in hand as all the while noting the hatches I see and the gobblers I hear from the roost. My fly fishing not to be any different, I notice each turkey and deer track along the streams, each fly-down gobble during a dawn hatch, and the trails to-and-from water in which I cross. It's a cycle of never-ending observation, in which each pursuit supports the other.

Yet, there is also that time in which I tend to focus most of all on my tying bench. It generally begins immediately after the Christmas rush, and goes right up to my spring gobbler scouting. January through April is when I can focus undistracted on my tying. The restocking of boxes takes place, a few patterns created from my notes during the previous season, and at times an article or two arises from the ashes in which I submit hopefully to the editors in charge. It's a time of leisure. No pressure to be had or timelines to be met....just my vise, the usual new materials from Christmas to play with and possibly a glass of local Merlot or Guinness to

One Small Trout

accompany me. The dogs tend to lie around at my feet as well. However, I'm not sure whether it's my presence and company that draws them in or the multitude of furs and feather scents that happens to be the main attractant? Either way, I'll take it.

I have found over the years that my winter tying is often the most productive as well. More of the patterns that have proven successful seem to come from winter sessions for me. Possibly because my time at the bench is less distracted by the wants, needs and desires of current hatches? Or knee-jerk reactions to on-stream hunches for needed changes to existing patterns. In the winter I can take a far more objective look at my boxes. I can step back from the time on the water and honestly look at a given pattern or idea. I find myself culling patterns that a season or more ago I was so excited about. Or looking at a given pattern and realizing that once the tail was chewed off, it did much better, prompting a revision. I also tend to tie a new pattern in 2-3 versions, and let the empty and full bins tell the tale for the future. I often find myself dumping my first pick into the reclaim bin, which is a process that I find to be quite humbling to say the least.

Just as I long for no interruptions to my other pursuits, so goes my winter tying as well; save for the periodic breaks for snow-blowing and the spreading of salt. I will often pass up time on the water for a day of tying during the winter months. Not because of weather or a lack of wanting to fish, but because my heart really just isn't in it. It belongs to my vise at those times, and when the winter snows come I am looking forward to it just as much as the start of any other season.

Influences

Sitting on an old trestle long abandoned by a defunct railway and now a historic pathway for trout fishermen, I looked at the water below my dangling legs as it passed silently by. I had fished through the morning and had enjoyed a relaxing, successful time on the water. A solid handful of fish had willingly risen to my offerings whenever I was able to put together a decent presentation, and there's really not much more that a person can ask for in my mind. No huge fish, but none were what one would consider small either. Just a good day....that is, in the eyes of this fisherman anyway. The end result? I was as happy-as-a-clam and content with the world.

R.E. Long

Now I found myself, as is an all too familiar habit of mine, pondering how I had gotten to this state of mind. I was not in a bad state, mind you. I was actually in a particularly good place, yet a place I would have expected had I just landed a 20+ inch wild fish, or had a record day on the water. Neither of which had happened. I had experienced a good morning on good water, with moderate success. But things just couldn't have felt better. So as I said, I sat there pondering why. Not that I was in a mood to give any of it back. No sir. I was perfectly content with my "place". I was just being myself and wanting to know just how I had gotten there, maybe so I could knowingly place myself there again; maybe somewhere downstream along the rest of my journey, when it was especially needed. So I sat; kicking my feet like a 12 year old, and looking upstream out over the water.

Thinking about it, I couldn't help but think of my Dad. He always seemed to "glaze over" when he neared a trout stream. He could walk by a million ponds and never toss a line. But let him stand along a trout stream and that current always seemed to sweep him away. I think I inherited that ailment, although, unlike my dad I can get the same way on a bluegill pond as well. My Mom gets the blame for my wanderlust. At a very young age, while growing up in the country, we would leave the house alone as children at sun-up not to return until dinner time most days. She instilled the idea of "no

One Small Trout

schedules" and the need to see what lies over the next hill and always had time for us to show or tell her about our adventures. Yet while it had helped my fishing over the years, it is a trait not always looked upon in a favorable light through much of life. My family has taught me moderation. Admittedly, I have been a horrible pupil at times. But they have taught me that one must appreciate each minute you get on the water, and to be content with stopping, even if it is for a recital of tone-deaf 14 year olds. No longer am I like the puppy that gets loose and has an uncontrollable need to sniff and mark a mile of telephone poles before coming to a stop in exhaustion and having to figure out just where the hell I am. These days when I get loose I head straight for the pole I enjoy the most, mark, then sit down and take it all in while appreciating the experience. Some call it a natural mellowing that comes with age. But I don't feel mellow or old. And besides, I see too many folks much older than I am now still chasing around the streams with fish counters and getting in near fist-fights over who had the right-of-way to a particular pool. I think it's something else.

I thought back to another time when this same feeling had taken over, and oddly enough the moment came back to me in vivid recollection. I was standing in the Skookumchuck River in Western Washington nearly 20 years ago, just downstream of my good friend Troy as we fished for spring-run Steelhead. It was cold and raining, but the temps were barely a few degrees above snow. We had fish holding in the pool we stood over, but neither of us had hooked any of them. What we had hooked were a few whitefish and a couple of smallish sea-run cutthroat, and though nice to catch, they were not exactly what we had come to catch. Though we were dressed expecting rain and the elements, it was one of those saturating days when at some point no matter how prepared you were you look up and realize that every inch of your being is wet and numb. Troy had just landed and released another whitefish when he looked downstream at me in a blank stare, paused and then said flatly, "These rocks hurt my feet." We both stood laughing in the ice cold water, with rain pouring off the brims of our hats. Fact is, neither of us could feel our feet any longer, and in the state of physical misery we were in, our feet were the least affected. Then without even sharing a word, we both turned and waded out of the water and back to my truck. We chose not to get out of our waders right away, and instead flopped down the tailgate and hopped up on it to pour a couple coffees from our lukewarm thermos. Sitting there in silence, sipping black coffee in the rain and watching the water roll by I recall having the same feeling.

The two moments however, only had one thing in common. In both, I was sitting on the water with my feet dangling. Maybe I was looking in the wrong direction. Maybe it's not so much the influences in our

One Small Trout

lives that affect our outlook on fishing. Maybe, it's the influence of spending time on the water that influences our outlook on life.

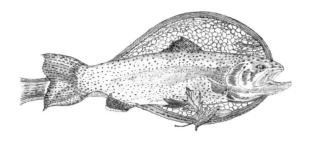

One Small Trout

<u>Yella Dog</u>

    I have very few streamer patterns in my box, simply because when one works I am prone to stick with it. But last season a particular pattern made it in, for one very good reason.....it worked. The Yella Dog is a simple pattern to tie, as far as Rangeley style patterns go. But sometimes simplicity is the key. I've found over the years that color matters. And sometimes that color is yellow.

Yella Dog Recipe

Hook: #10 Daiichi 2370 Dick Talleur

Thread: 8/0 Black Uni-thread

Rib: Medium Gold Tinsel

Body: Yellow Uni-floss

Under-wing: Red Bucktail

Over-Wing: 4 Pheaasant tail fibers

Throat: Red Tippet

Wing: Opposing Yellow-dyed Badger Brahma Hackles

Shoulder: Yellow-Dyed Indian Hackles

One Small Trout

Tying Instructions

1- Tie in the tinsel about one eye-length behind the eye, and wrap back to a point even with the barb of the hook.

2- Bring the thread back to the tie-in point and tie in the floss, wrapping back to a point even with the point of the hook.

3- Form an even body with the floss toward the front of the hook, tying off at the original start point.

4- Wrap the tinsel forward up the shank to the rear of the floss, then palmer an even rib forward, tie off and add a small amount of head cement at the tie off point.

5- Tie in the red tippet on the underside of the hook with the tips extending to the mid- point of the shank.

6- Tie in a sparse bunch of red bucktail on the top of the hook extending back to point 2 gap-lengths past the bend of the hook.

7- Tie in the pheasant tail fibers arching over the olive bucktail, extended to the same point.

8- Apply a small amount of head cement or superglue to the tie in point, whip finish.

Prepare the wing

9- Identify two opposing Brahma hackles of a length that once the base of the quill is stripped of webbing will extend to the same point as the red bucktail.

10- Identify 2 opposing hen Indian hackles with the white center-line and evenly strip the quills clean.

11- Using a dab of super glue or head cement marry and attach each indian hackle feather to the appropriate brahma hackle.

12- Once dry, mount each assembled wing/shoulder to the appropriate side of the hook.

13- Build a clean tapered head, whip finish and apply desired head cement.

Little Rings

Standing on the bank of the pond offered an elevated perch from which to observe the body of waters world which was laid out in full display. The late august sun was but a short distance from the horizon and the air, heavily laden with moisture, hung on my shoulders like a blanket. The air was filled with the metallic blues and greens of dozens of damsel flies, along with their larger cousins the dragon fly, coursed over the water's surface creating an ever-moving tapestry. Easing my way along the bank with my eye on a small pocket of lily pads towards the shallow end of the pond where the springs filtered into the small depression, I spotted a painted turtle just seconds before my presence was discovered and it slipped off a branch disappearing beneath the surface algae. A bullfrog set a solid cadence from within the cattails as I approached and startled a dozen or so red-winged black-birds which noisily took flight. The bullfrog's cadence was silenced with the departure of the birds, but quickly resumed after a short minute. What had remained a constant however, were the small rings on the surface that were rhythmically appearing in amongst the lily pads. That was my quarry.

It was one of those lazy summer days which just felt right to punctuate with an ending that included a fly rod, and this small body of water was but a hop-skip-and-a-jump from my home. So armed with a small box of size 10 hair poppers and a spool of 5x tippet, I was in pursuit of what lay below those rings upon the water. Easing into position to start working the outer edge of the lily pads, the customary "plop, plop" of small leopard frogs signaled that I had indeed "arrived". The rings were such that they could be the result of anything from a 3 inch bluegill on up to a big slab of a gill. The latter is what I had my hopes on since about every dozen rings one would be accompanied with a "snick" of a noise which told me that something of somewhat substantial size was feeding amongst them at the very least. The click-pawl of my single action reel announced

One Small Trout

the start of the games as my first half dozen false casts
shook the dust off my shoulder. The small popper lit on
the surface just shy of the pads and was greeted
instantly with the pop of a fish. My immediate reflex
was to set the hook much too quickly and in effect
ripped the fly away from the hungry fish much to my
frustration. The fish had however, revealed itself as a
palm sized bluegill. Still laughing at myself for the
rookie mistake, I dropped another cast in about the
same spot and watched as the rings of its impact
dissipated. It only took seconds however for it to
disappear as it was sucked in leaving a small ½" bubble
of air at the surface in its place.

With the initial lift of the rod my first thought
was that it had already wrapped my leader in the stalks
of the vegetation, but as I held pressure high the telltale
sign of life came with a deep pulsing of a heavier fish
than expected. Putting pressure on it to keep my line
out of the lilies as much as possible, I worked the fish
down the bank into deeper water and turned to wearing
it out. My 7 foot 4-weight rod was getting a workout as I
fought through 3 or 4 good solid pulsing runs. Then as
suddenly as the fight had begun, it was over. The fish let
me glide it to the bank with only a half-hearted half-
circle of a run as its last gasp of effort. Lifting the fish, its
weight was apparent immediately. A full 1-inch thick at
the back and nearly 7-inches back-to-belly, it was an
impressive bluegill. The back was solid black, fading to

near silver on the flanks, and then exploding into a dark copper breast. And in stark contrast to the copper breast lay an almost jet-black gill spot glistening in the sun. A beautiful male that rivaled any bluegill I had hooked to date. The fish lay in my hand perfectly still as I admired it, never so much as even moving a gill plate. But as I placed it back into the shallow water of the bank it instantly exploded with energy, splashing water and disappearing in the blink of an eye.

I rinsed my hands and gathered my rod together, then walked back up to sit on the bank for a bit and take in the moment. Looking back out over the pond again I tended to the battered little popper that had just done its duty so well. Blowing on the hackle-tip tailing I quickly had the little fly back in working order and ready for more. Recalling the patch of caribou hair that had spawned its existence in the jaws of my vise only the day prior, it seemed almost poetic that a bit of natural material such as caribou hair and rooster feathers had brought to hand such a beautiful fish. Having fished this pond a number of times in the past, I had seldom landed anything much larger than palm-sized fish in my efforts. This fish had been a huge surprise, and a welcome one. On the water, the small rings on the surface had begun again. I smiled thinking how such a small nearly insignificant disturbance on the surface of the water, had kept hidden such an impressive fish. I sat there watching the water, deciding

One Small Trout

not to wet my line again, as the last of the sun dipped below the horizon and the sounds of the birds and cicadas were replaced by peepers and crickets. What I had come looking for had already been found, and I chose to end the night without clouding the memory of an exceptional fish among those little rings.

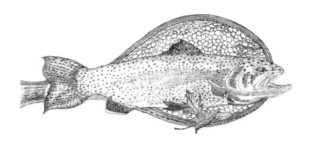

The Spider Hole

The chest-high weeds were thick and held the heat at an oppressive level as I pushed my way towards the edge of the water. The pinelands of southern New Jersey in late September can get hot, and this week was no exception. I had stumbled on a small spring-fed pothole while scouting for archery season a few weeks prior, and had promised myself to check it out with the fly rod. On my first visit I could see swirls of what appeared to be larger fish all across the small pond, but the tea-stained water of the cedar swamps would not give me a glimpse of just what it was feeding below the surface. On top of that the weeds grew to the water's edge and nowhere would I find any sort of casting lane.

So today I came prepared, toting my old donut float-tube and fins in order to get away from the bank.

Upon my arrival, it appeared my tube had made the ride through the briars and wait-a-minute vines since it still held air, which was a good sign to start the day. The only bad part of the trip in, were the masses of large yellow and orange striped garden spiders that were spread out across every game trail opening I crossed. As I rigged up I found myself wiping off nearly a half-dozen of the big lumbering critters as they clung to my waders and tube. Spiders are not my favorite bug in the world, but this particular spider is so commonplace that they become like a horsefly buzzing your head; more irritating than truly bothersome. I stomped out an area of weeds largest enough to set my tube down and ready my gear. I had worn my old Redball non-breathable waders for this foray, and now the effects of their durability had begun to collect its taxes as the dark brown material began to heat up inside. Feeling the heat grow put urgency into getting in my fins, with a much anticipated feeling of sitting in the cooler water. As I scurried about in my little cove, I began to laugh at myself. Have you ever put socks on the legs of your dog as a youngster just to see how they will react and walk? Well, no need. Just go watch a tube fisherman move around in kick fins and try to get in his tube and into the water. Both the dog and the fisherman react and move in pretty much the same manner. Yet in

One Small Trout

the end, I found myself floating in cool water, dripping sweat and slowly finning towards the middle of the small body of water to take in my surroundings and rig my gear.

Not fishing my heavy bass gear today, I had grabbed my 5-weight Far-and-Fine on the way out the door. I didn't expect to encounter anything really huge in the little piece of water, so I rigged with a 9 foot 3X leader and looped on a 3 foot section of 5x fluorocarbon tippet. I decided to begin with a purple mohair leach with a purple marabou tail. Nothing too big, just tied on a size 10 standard streamer hook. Stripping out line on the apron of the tube, I could see the same swirls near the weed edges all around the pond. The bank was just out of reach from the center, but if I moved about 10 feet in any direction a simple haul would put me right on the weeds-edge. And that's where I began.

On my first cast the streamer hit in the thin algae a few feet from the bank. I gave the fly a slow count of 3, and then began my retrieve. On about the 4th strip my fly was hammered, nearly ripping the rod out of my hand as it caught me off-guard! Then after a couple headshakes, it was gone with my fly. "Holy Crap!" I said out loud with nobody but myself around to listen, "I'm going to need a larger tippet." I re-rigged with a slight tremble of excitement in my hands, looping on another 3 feet of 3X fluorocarbon and adding another purple leach. On my second cast of the morning my fly made it halfway back to the tube when it was again slammed from a large fish beneath the surface of the dark water. This time however, the leader held. And shortly into the battle it was apparent that I was playing a pickerel. But it was a large pickerel! As I finally wore it out and slid its duck-bill shaped mug up onto my apron I was surprised at its girth. I was looking at an 18 inch Chain pickerel, with a body that more resembled a musky than a pickerel. Its belly was nearly 4 inches top-to-bottom. It was a real brute that was obviously eating quite well amongst the cedars. Pleased with the catch, I am not a fan of pickerel for the table, so I bid the hefty little bugger a 'due, and back into the water it went. I wondered just what else would be in here, as I spun myself 180degrees to try the other bank. What else would thrive with teeth like that swimming in here? My answer came quickly, as the next 10 casts landed 6 more fish nearly identical to the first. I was in 7th heaven as I grinned like a Cheshire cat with each fish. I believe I landed over 20 fish before a nature call and the need for water drove me back to the bank. By that time the heat of the day was peaking, so back to the car I went while planning my next visit to the little honey-hole. After storing my gear in the truck, I was sitting looking out the windshield waiting for the air-conditioning to kick in while drinking a lukewarm bottle of water. When there it was, another one of those big garden spiders lumbering across my dash behind the steering wheel!

One Small Trout

Quickly I escorted his creepy little 8 legged nemesis out of my truck in none-too-kind fashion. AGH….I hate spiders!

That was six years ago, and I still try to hit the "Spider Hole" a couple times a year. It's much more productive on wet years, as discovery has shown that it is really an overflow pond from a small estuary about 200-yards through the woods. It appears that in periods of properly timed high water the baitfish rush into that small channel, and then become landlocked. In those wet years, the Pickerel are huge and the fishing is great. On dry years it is average and the pickerel are thin. But there always seems to be plenty of spiders.

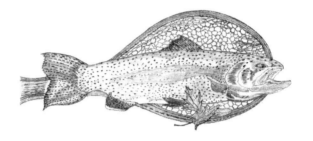

<u>Gordy</u>

The Gordy was born in my vise about 4 years ago and was named at that time due to the Quill body used resembling the Quill Gordon. It is a proven performer on most all of the waters across Pennsylvania, as well as some of Virginia. This pattern excels under an indicator as an all-around search pattern.

Gordy Recipe

Hook: #18-#14 Standard Scud Hook

Thread: 8/0 Brown Uni-Thread

Bead: Gold Tungsten

Abdomen: Peacock Quill coated with Bug Bond

Thorax: Dark Dun Orvis Spectrablend / Peacock Ice-Dub

Wingcase: Dark Brown Turkey Biots

One Small Trout

<u>Tying Instructions</u>

1- Apply 5 wraps of lead wire behind bead and seat firmly behind the bead.

2- Start your thread behind the lead wraps and over-wrap the lead to secure.

3- Tie in one stripped peacock herl behind bead and wrap back to a point in line with the barb of the hook.

4- Bring your thread forward building a slightly tapered underbody.

5- Wrap peacock herl forward to the bead and tie off. Coat with a thin layer of Bug Bond.

6- Dub a small section of Spectrablend at the rear half of the thorax.

7- Tie in Turkey Biots in a delta over the Spectrablend.

8- Dub the forward portion of the thorax with Ice-Dub and whip finish.

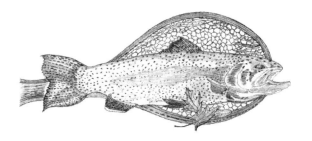

Gathering Hackle

The loud double-gobble broke the silence of the pre-dawn air, raising the hair on my forearms with adrenalin and instantly increasing my heart rate. Without hesitation I knew I needed to close the distance as fast and quietly as I could before the roosted gobbler decided to drop down and walk away with his hens. It was opening day for New Jerseys Spring Gobbler season and I was excited for 2 reasons. First, I simply can't get enough of chasing Gobblers. It's in my blood and part of who I am. And secondly, it is by far the single most fun fly tying material excursion of the year.

The Eastern Wild Turkey at first glance appears almost black when viewed from a distance. Yet up close they are a beautiful display of metallic copper, bronze & greens that only nature can produce. A single bird will provide more hackle than the average fly tyer can utilize in a lifetime of tying, however the best part is sharing among friends and then renewing the supply each spring season. For my own purposes, nearly the entire bird is put to use. The meat is obviously used, which to me is one of the best eating game birds found anywhere. The primary feathers on the wings are kept, split and ground for custom arrow fletching among myself and friends. The wing bones are used for wing-bone turkey calls, which are an art that I am getting "somewhat" proficient at over the years. And then my efforts turn towards plucking the most useful feathers to stock my bench.

The most obvious hackles are the tail feathers of the gobbler, which are used for everything from hopper wing-cases to beetle shells, caddis wings, and a myriad of additional applications. Both natural and shellacked, I tend to consume them at a high rate throughout a season. Next are the secondary wing feathers or what are commonly referred to as "mottled turkey rounds". Most popular as the winging material for muddler minnows, they are another staple on a bench that tends to become a regular purchase for an active tyer. With 4-6 of them per side, they become a premium for matched pairs. After that I move on to the flats. The three most used flats on my bench are the barred, the copper & the

One Small Trout

green. All have their applications, from streamer wings to classic wets and nymph bodies their uses are only limited by your imagination. The most valuable hackle to my bench however are the soft-hackles found on the outer side of the lower legs. They are a naturally barred hackle ranging from #12 to #8 that I have never found anywhere in a fly shop. They are perfect for Carey Specials, steelhead and streamer collars and large nymph legging. Their attributes are very much like a Hungarian partridge hackle, but a bit more durable in my opinion. Each leg gives up about the same amount of hackle as one would find in a standard dubbing packet. To me, they are the gold found on every eastern wild turkey.

Though it may not be so for every fly tyer, I find the satisfaction of catching a fish on a pattern that I not only tied, but harvested the materials in which it was tied with to be that much more enjoyable. It is an aspect that helps to bring me full-circle in my outdoor pursuits. Add to that the sharing of patterns that others tie with those same hackles and the gifts from a single gobbler are endless.

So on this morning, as luck would have it, the hunting gods were on my side. That double gobble was not just a single turkey, but a trio of gobblers bent on a battle of the strut. The ghost of the morning mist materialized from the cedar grove from which it had first gobbled, with antagonists in trail. I admired them as they displayed their plumage with heart-pounding exhilaration as gobble after gobble they put on a display for that unseen hen in the timber. It wasn't until the lead bird broke from the group and turned in my direction that I found my opening, and shortly thereafter stood over a gift of nature's fly shop. There would be an amazing dinner to be had. And there would be countless flies tied as a result of this gathering of hackle.

Home Waters

This past year, when compared to my normal years on the water, was a struggle for time. On average I try to get out once a week on at least some type of water. But this year brought a new home relocation and health issues, along with a daughter deploying overseas. So time was at a premium along with a priority shift. The trips out west were postponed, and most of the planned overnighters were changed to day trips on home water. Yet although during the ordeal I was often left chomping at the bit, upon reflection it was far from a negative year. The streams were still inviting, the fish were still there and when I was able to present a fly properly they even rose every now and then to eat one. Who can possibly find fault in that?

R.E. Long

Over time we can tend to glaze over as we drive by home waters. Along with familiarity one often finds boredom following close behind. Not necessarily because the fishing is poor, but rather because we tend to look over those yonder blue mountains and imagine greener pastures and larger fish. So we travel. And whether the fishing proves to be better or not, we become enthralled in the romance of the journey as much as the fish catching. To be walking a new stream in awe of the never seen before scenery, we wonder at what may lie in each pool we encounter. There is no memory of the fish you once hooked by "that old deadfall", or the fish that took you into the "pool below". That in itself tends to make a person fish water much more thorough since there are no preconceived notions about where the fish will be found.

This was cemented into my consciousness on a trip this past fall to water that I have been fishing since my childhood. I found that I had about three hours of time with no other wants-needs-or desires from any outside influences, so off I ran with a quickness to take advantage. It is a slower stream often affected by the summer heat, but the cooling of fall should have improved things. And the normal summer crowds should have subsided. Or at least I hoped. I had fished several pools above the access point, and had been rewarded with a few smallish but beautiful browns. Then as I had on countless times over the years on

One Small Trout

previous trips, I stepped off into the brush to go around the pool ahead that took me into a cow pasture. Why? Just out of habit mainly. In past years I had been skunked there more often than not, so I had begun writing that pool off. So for many years, it was a "no fish zone" in my mind. But on this day after settling into the water in the pool just upstream, I looked down to see rise-forms. I stood there watching for a few minutes, and there they were again. A pod of fish seemed to be regularly working in the pool. The pool with no fish in it! Being stubborn by nature, but not always foolish, I made a quick about-face and made my way back through the brush to the tail-out of the pool. In short order I was in position to cast upstream to the head of the pool and waited. It took about 10 minutes, then just as I was about to tell myself "I told you so" and head back upstream, there they were.

The next 2 hours found me in the same place. After landing close to a dozen fish on an Elk-Hair Caddis dry, I switched to a Squirrels Nest nymph and pulled another dozen fish off the bottom! I had no reason to move and right about the time the bite began to slow, I realized that I had just enough time to get back to the truck and home before turning back into a pumpkin. On the drive home my mind kept going back to that pool. Trip after trip over the years I had fished that pool, and NEVER so much as caught a single fish. So my mind had written that piece of water off. How many times had I done that? I began to dig into my subconscious and think back to sections that I had been walking past for much the same reason on other waters. There were others. And as I catalogued them away, I decided to end that bad habit going forward. The move proved to be a good one. Where familiarity had embedded negative impressions of certain waters, I had begun walking past otherwise productive waters. Mainly due to the fact that I had personally not been able to crack the code of a particular pool or run. That is something that does not happen on new water. On new water you dredge and drift every likely productive looking lie you come upon. Along with otherwise non-productive looking lies that are just within reach at the time. Many of which prove to be holding nice fish. We never second guess those times because, as is the case many times, fish are simply "where you find them". Which is something that we know and accept as common knowledge normally, yet often ignore on home waters.

The result of this season; I reconnected with a few waters that I had not fished in many years. Waters that I would drive over and ignore on many trips elsewhere began to take on a new light. I found new pools, new access points and in many cases fish where I had never before found them. They were not new waters in reality, but with a fresh approach and a new outlook they were again trips filled with the wonder of what the next pool would hold. Hopefully this upcoming

One Small Trout

year will provide a bit more time than the last. But even if it does, there is still a bucket list on my tying bench of home waters that are due up next for another visit. Those long trips may just have to wait a bit when the weather warms.

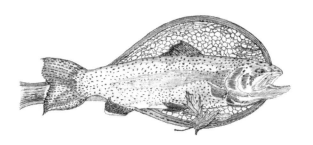

<u>The Guinness Trout</u>

There are times when a pattern is born far away from any body of water. This is just such a pattern. This pattern began as a twinkling in the eye at a Tying Conclave, as I watched a freshly poured glass of Guinness Stout settle to a head.....the dark chocolate undertones of the beer against the caramel bubbles rising to form a creamy tan head, as seen through a glass wearing a gold harp. The sight not only made me thirsty, but it took my sense of humor to the vise as well.

119

But here is the best part. That event took place three winters ago, and since then the Guinness Trout has been hammered repeatedly while dead-drifted deep, below an indicator. As with the beer, sometimes you just can't ignore something that works.

Guinness Trout Recipe

Hook: #8 Standard Streamer

Thread: 6/0 Rusty Dun Uni-thread

Bead head: 1/8" Tungsten

Abdomen: Tying Thread

Tail: Tan Marabou

Hackle: Furnace dry hackle

Rib: Fine Gold Wire

One Small Trout

Tying Instructions

1- Wrap .015 lead wire from mid-shank to behind the bead, and seat well.

2- Start thread behind the lead wraps and overwrap to secure.

3- Bring the thread back to the barb and tie in the marabou tips to form a tail shank length and trim butts just behind the lead wraps.

4- Tie in the gold wire just behind the lead wraps.

5- Sweep a large base hackle from the tips back and trim off the light brown tip of the furnace hackle.

6- Tie in the hackle tip-first at the tail with shiny side forward.

7- Build a level thread body forward all the way up to the bead.

8- Palmer the hackle forward to the bead, secure but do not trim.

9- Counter wrap the wire forward to the bead and trim excess.

10-Wrap the webbed base of the remaining hackle to form a heavy collar, trim and whip finish.

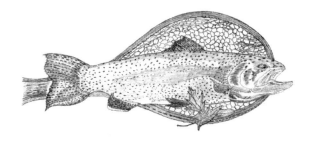

Children

For most of us fishing, let alone fly fishing, is a progression. Most come to fishing in the same manner that includes a spinning or spin-cast rod and reel, a bobber and some form of bait. Not all, but most. It's the period where hooking fish is not really the paramount objective in the journey, but rather the hooking of the child to the outdoors and fishing that matters most. Many never leave this form of fishing, and happily for them so-be-it. We all attempt to get what we need as an individual from the outdoors and it's a very personal journey. Somewhere along the line many of us either merge into a specific form of fishing, or a specific target fish. This in itself can have a major effect on our fishing progression. If your passion pulls you to warm-water fishing, more often than not that will influence a person's choices of rod and reel. The normal progression is toward bait-casting and lures, with the possibility of a niche passion for the fly rod. Likewise, if your passion draws you towards blue-water and Bluefin tuna, you're probably not going to find a short transition to the fly rod in your future; if ever. Trout seem to be the main deciding factor in a somewhat faster transition to the fly rod. It is where most of the gear is targeted, and where the vast majority of fly fishermen seem to naturally migrate. Never-the-less, the fly rod is not a final step, nor is it a guarantee to draw a person in regardless of the years spent fishing. It just tends to happen in somewhat of a progressive nature when it does.

Over this past years' holiday season I was fortunate to have all of my children in my home at some point. And it gave me time to sit back and remember their first fish, the smiles on their faces, and where they went as they grew up. My oldest daughter cut her teeth on Mt St. Helens area trout on a spinning rod. She did well and truly enjoyed it. Yet the fishing bug never really bit her hard enough to pull her through her teens. Her two sisters both broke into grins over stocked trout in Northern Pennsylvania. Like any child that hooks a fish, the delight and smiles were invaluable both to them and me as well. Yet, the bug that bit me as a youth did not take hold. My son, who is the youngest, has been busy catching bluegills and trout with worms and a spinning rod. It appears that when he is fishing he loves it, but when not fishing it may as well not even exist. The attention span is just not there, which is normal for a 10 year old. This past year he asked for a fly rod and spent 2 days fishing with it. Who knows whether or not the bug will bite him down the road. They all have dabbled in fly tying over time, but not to the extent of their father, who by all accounts may have been bitten much too hard and by something nearly lethal. But the natural curiosity did surface, and the seeds were planted.

Where things have differed, has been during the summer vacation where family merges and the beach is a common theme. With the beach comes surf fishing, both day and night. No fly rod is employed, but a multitude of sand spikes are, stuffed with large spinning tackle and cut bait. It is here that young and old all come together as if they are all five years old again, catching everything from sharks, to skates and rays, bluefish, stripers, spot and fluke. This for us is where those early planted seeds begin to blossom and the smiles return. They are all once again yelling for "Dad" to unhook the skates that nobody else will touch. They have replaced the worms of their childhood. So I do, and I run up and down the beach building memories as I go. Maybe someday they will come to me and say, "Dad, I want to learn how to fly fish." Maybe a boyfriend or co-worker who fishes will get them thinking about it, and their minds will drift back to the childhood smiles and that alone may prompt them to give it a try. Maybe after I'm gone, they will sit back with one of my books and recall sitting on a stream bank or standing in surf, and they'll smile once more in remembrance. Or quite possibly it won't hit them until they see their own child's smile, grinning ear-to-ear at a palm-sized bluegill.

I felt at one point that I would steer them towards fly fishing, and somehow they would feel what I felt when on the water, but soon decided that it had to be on their own terms. Someday I hope they all get to experience the rush of water against waders as their fly disappears in a swirl and the rod is lifted to meet the weight of a fish. You just never know. I'll still continue to nudge them either way. And regardless of the outcome; they fished.

Bobbers

The cold water was a welcome feeling on my legs as I eased my way out into the current. With nearly a month gone-by since I had last held a rod, it was a long overdue sensation as well as a much needed bit of therapy. The recent weeks had brought with it many obstacles, from the stresses of life and its ailments to the annual archery season; the result was my fly rods had been collecting dust. But life's ailments were easing a bit and I had a fat doe in the freezer compliments of the local oak ridges, so it was time. Having rigged at the truck for the walk into the stream I was ready to go. In my hand was my Far-and-Fine, lined with a 5-weight double-taper line, 5 foot furled mono leader and 4 foot of 5x fluorocarbon tippet. My fly of choice was a size14 Squirrels Nest. All that remained was my indicator, of which I chose a yellow half inch Thing-a-ma-bobber and looped it into my leader just above the tippet ring. A quick glance upstream and my roll-cast flipped the rig to the head of the riffle.

The first few drifts were uneventful as I slowly became part of the scene, the rhythm of the indicator dancing along the current like hypnosis for the weary and unaccustomed mind. Had there been a strike, I probably would have missed it. Then on about the 5th cast I noticed to late the slight dip in the indicator and my lift of the rod proved fruitless. OK. Enough of that as my mind finally caught up to my current place in the world. "I saw you", I thought to myself out loud, and as my indicator drift over the same spot for a second time I was much quicker in reflex. My reward was a fat 12 inch brown trout dancing on the end of my line with the little gold bead-head fly tucked tightly in the corner of his jaw. I short fight in the colder water and in moments I was admiring his colors. Although not the buttery gold of a summer or early fall fish, his silver flanks with distinct black spotting made up for the faded orange ones in which they surrounded. It was almost as if nature had stripped away the color along with the falling of the leaves, leaving only the silvery-grey and metallic hues much like the bare branches of the tree themselves. In all things there is beauty to be seen however, so I admired the change for what it was and

One Small Trout

smiled as the fish slipped from my hand and returned to its lie amongst the streams rocky bottom.

Turning back to my rod I noticed my indicator had become entangled a bit and struggled with cold fingers to free it of its malady. In the end it became easier to simply remove it and then untangle the leader itself, and as I did so I inadvertently dropped the little plastic ball into the stream. With what probably looked like a bout of stationary panic to the casual observer, I nearly fell over in my scramble to catch the rapidly escaping indicator before it was gone forever. Unable to do so however, I stood and watched it dance off towards waters unknown, lost forever. I laughed at myself for my moment of scramble. I probably looked just as I had as a youth dropping a bobber off the side of a deck on the local pond, where I would stand helplessly staring over the edge at it below me after a short juggling act, so close, but out of my reach short of an unwanted plunge. Yet here I was doing the same routine years later. Had I changed so little as to react just the same some 50 years later? I would like to think not. Surely I'm now light years beyond that small boy with a spinning rig and bobber! After all, I was now a fly fisherman! I no longer even used bobbers! I thought about that as I looked down at the small zip-lock bag of indicators in my hand. Something told me that quite possibly the only person fooled was myself. Miniature bobbers stared back at me. On the package it said strike indicator with "trapped air technology". It appeared to me however, to be the exact same thing as was that red-and-white plastic bobber back in 1968 on a small farm pond in Pennsylvania. I reckon I really had not come all that far after all I thought to myself. I could hear my dad's voice in my ear again saying, "You're walking a little slow boy, but you're catching up." His normal response for whenever I was having trouble grasping the obvious. "Yeah, yeah, I hear ya." I answered out loud as I roll-cast upstream once more, smiling despite myself. The next cast brought with it another slight dip of the indicator and yet again the weight of a fish which was a near perfect minting of the 1st. As I popped the hook from its jaw and released the fish the thought on my mind slipped from my lips without thinking. "I could do this all day", I said as the words sort of caught me off guard. Maybe the fact was that I had never really gone beyond that young boy when it came to being on the water after all? Or maybe I had just come full-circle. Either way, I was content. Taking a couple steps downstream, I flipped my rig upstream once more and watched that little yellow bobber dance along the current.

M&M

The M&M Nymph is short for "My Moose Nymph". It was tied originally for the Yellow Breeches on mid-winter trips. I've held this pattern close-to-the-vest for a number of years, and its been a trip saver more often than not. Fished on an indicator and deep, this pattern does extremely well. I do fairly well with it throughout the year as a caddis larva also, but it truly shines in the winter.

The M&M Recipe

Hook: #18 Beadhead

Bead: Gold Tungsten

Thread: 6/0 Black Uni-thread

Abdomen: Moose body hair

Hackle: Furnace Hen Hackle

Collar: Black Ice-Dub

One Small Trout

<u>Tying Instructions</u>

1- Apply 5 wraps of fine lead wire behind bead and seat firmly behind the bead.

2- Start your thread behind the lead wraps and over-wrap the lead to secure.

3- Tie in two Moose body hairs behind bead and wrap back to a point in line with the barb of the hook.

4- Bring your thread forward building a slightly tapered underbody transitioning into the lead.

5- Wrap both Moose body hair forward side-by-side to the bead and tie off. Coat with a thin layer of Bug Bond.

6- Tie in Furnace hackle shiny side forward and give two turns of hackle. Tie of and clip.

7- Dub Ice-Dub collar slightly forced back into the hackle.

8- Whip finish.

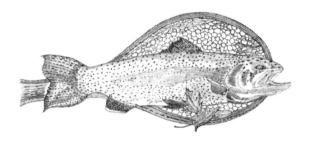

Bucktails

Closing the back hatch on the Xterra, I turned in clumsy wader boots fighting the loose gravel and headed for the water. It was an early spring morning and today I would be hunting trout. That's what I call streamer fishing when eventual meat for the table is the intended goal. To me it's back to the basics, tying on a traditional Bucktail streamer and pounding water in the places that experience has shown me the trout should be. It goes all the way back to my first days with a spinning rod, flicking CP Swings and Colorado spinners in their silver and gold hammered regalia. All it took was a decent amount of skill at placing your spinner where it needed to go, and the trout would respond. Later it would turn to a minnow bucket or Salt minnows on minnow rigs. I can still hear my Dad wading next to

135

me and pointing out where to cast and how to get the best drift. He was first-and-foremost a minnow fisherman and always seemed able to pull big fish out of the most unlikely places. I would stumble along beside him and emulate him to the best of my ability, casting in the same manner and standing "just so". Back then I never thought he could see me copying him, but now that I have kids of my own I realize he certainly did. I hope it made him smile as well, just as it does me now with my children.

Today however, I would be carrying a fly rod, as I have pretty much exclusively for many years. I have not lost the love for drifting minnows as a practice, but seldom ever do. Finding it simpler and just as effective with my bucktails, I choose the grace of my 6 weight these days. I began the morning with a Northwest Jack. It's a pattern of my own along the same lines as a Black-nosed Dace, and my streamer of choice for northeast stocked fish. It began life as a larger Steelhead streamer, hence the name, but seemed to perform the best over the years as a smaller trout streamer as it doubles nicely for both a salmon smolt and a shiner imitation. The mini sink-tip line flipped the short foot fluorocarbon leader with perfection as I worked the first run and on my 10th or 12th cast the fly came to a jolting stop. Not a big fish, but a perfectly minted 12 inch rainbow came to hand and placed the day in the books as the first fish. While not necessary to have a

One Small Trout

successful day on the water, not getting skunked is a good thing in my book and the first fish is always a welcomed event. I admired the fish which was still in its winter colors, with reds more of a burnt orange and the dark olive back blending into the light gray & lacking that summer silver. Or maybe it was just the overcast day and no sun to dance on its flank that caused it to look as such. Nevertheless it was beautiful all the same and it brought a smile as the last thrust of its tail took it from my hand. And now with a taste of victory on my tongue the mood swung back to the hunt. No leisurely stroll along the creek today. This was all purpose, stalking the holes and runs, casting at targets, putting my fly where I wanted it instead of drifting by the current; all in a much more aggressive tone of fishing than a day of dry fly fishing. I was looking for a brace of fish in the 14 inch range, preferably browns, but any would do. The hunt took me upstream at a fairly rapid pace as I released several more smallish fish and examined my fly as it took a beating. Then, on the 3 third pool upstream I set the hook on a much nicer fish and soon brought to hand a fat 15 inch holdover brown. The weight of the fish in my creel was comforting as I pressed upstream. I had identified, by this point, the fish were looking for a "strip-pause" retrieve, and a much slower action. It continued to work as I moved further along, bringing several more fish to hand. It wasn't until I was nearly a mile from the truck that I set the hook on another heavy fish. This one took my bucktail as it dead-drifted down and across through a knee-deep rapid. It was a rainbow! A fact confirmed in the 1st of several spectacular jumps it put on display before finally tiring to my hand. I placed the second fish in my creel and looked up for the first time with something other than where my next cast would be on my mind. That's when I knew it was time to turn around. For nearly two hours I had remained "in the moment", which had left me tired yet extremely satisfied.

My walk back to the truck did not include fishing. I walked and reflected. I had fished this exact place many times with my Dad, and though much of the stream itself had changed over the many years of storms and floods, it still felt the same as when I barely filled a heavy pair of rubber hip-boots. It was a good walk, and one that was as satisfying as the day of fishing itself. I reached the bridge where I had parked and turned to climb up the slight grade to the parking area. Just as I reached the gravel of the parking lot, I was approached by another fisherman heading back down the same path. He carried a spinning rod and across his chest was slung an old worn Heddon minnow bucket. The bucket looked exactly like the one that sits on my shelf in my tying room today.

"Any luck" he asked?

"Yep" I responded with a smile, "More than I had expected."

One Small Trout

"Great news" he exclaimed! "I've been waiting for this day all winter."

"Good luck and enjoy the water" I replied as we both nodded to each other in passing and he dropped down the bank to the stream.

Continuing on to the back of my truck, I was removing my creel when it hit me. "Good luck and enjoy the water" was the very same response in passing that my Dad said each and every time he greeted another fisherman in passing. And you could tell when he said it that he truly meant it. Could it be that I was still stumbling along, emulating the man after so many years past? The thought brought a smile to my face at the memory. It had indeed been a good day on the water, and I would round it out with a brace of fresh trout and black coffee. Thanks Dad.

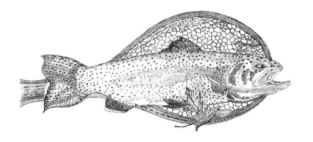

When Bass Get Bored

I pulled into the lake's public access lane and drove past the boat and trailer parking area, pausing out of surprise when I noticed there was not a single vehicle parked. Realizing that mid-August heat can often drive fishermen away, I expected to see at least a few early-birds such as myself on the water. From the looks of things however, there was not a single boat on the lake yet. My surprise was added to shortly thereafter upon finding even the lower parking area vacant as well. Could it be that I actually had the entire lake to myself? As I stood at my tailgate rigging my gear with a full view of three fourths of the lake I could not find a soul. The way I saw it, either I was the luckiest fisherman in the county on this morning, or the rest of

141

the folks already knew that recent fishing on this water stunk. I figured that optimism would be the best bet until proven otherwise.

Tying on a modest-sized deer hair popper of the Fruit Cocktail genre, I headed for the windward side of the lake where a high bank shielded the water. My target was the algae matting and calm coves formed along the curving bank. On approach the usual fleeing wakes of juvenile bluegills gave way to my presence. I was looking at a small 6 foot opening in the nearest algae mat and my 6 weight floating line was already airborne. The little popper landed with a splat in the middle of the opening, and I watched as the resulting rings grew, and then dissipated as they spread further from my offering. With no strike appearing right away, I gave the popper a short 2 inch twitch-retrieve. It was immediately slammed by a large open mouth, followed by a tail slap of defiance as if it was saying "Take that!" Elated by an early strike I was in my glory, as the 3 pound fish put on a strong showing before coming to hand. It was a nice fat-bellied fish to open the morning. Figuring it was just a lucky teaser to a morning of casting and searching; I accepted things willingly and moved down the bank towards a next opening. However, that was not to be the case. What I found was nearly a quarter mile of fish after fish, with hardly a cast failing to at least producing a strike. They were all two to three pound fish, and all hit like they had never seen a fly or lure before in their lives. Not quite the norm for this water from my past experiences. It was as-if they were all finning just under the algae, looking up in anticipation, knowing that I was getting closer to their location.

At one point I stopped to look around. What I saw was a single elderly couple. The wife was walking their small white miniature dog along the sunny, park side of the lake. The husband was sitting on a bench watching in my direction. Nothing else; no boats, no bank fishermen were to be found. Grateful for the solitude and quiet water I went back to business and proceeded along as before; searching out open pockets of algae and raising fish. The entire morning was exactly what I needed. I was in search of a day with no struggles or schedules, where I could unwind and hopefully catch a fish or two on the fly rod. It did not let me down. A long summer of projects and family events had absorbed most of my summer. Yet in a single morning, a single fish had erased all of that as I had gripped that first wet, green lip.

I reached the end of my wind-shielded cove and paused to look around once again, finding there was virtually no change. The section of lake in front of me held no refuge from the wind or any cover of algae. It would be a bit different approach for covering this water, most likely requiring a streamer of some sorts and some double-hauling towards deeper water. I chose to turn around. I was satisfied. My walk back was more a recollection of the fish I had just landed and released than anything else. The ever-changing algae still had some of the same openings in them, but new ones had formed as others had closed. I wondered if the bass had enjoyed the morning as well. It sure seemed like they had. They had hit with a complete lack of abandon like a Lab that has not chased a tennis ball in far too long, wanting only to drop the ball at your feet with tail wagging in anticipation of the next throw. Maybe they had needed this morning as much as I had?

Nearing my truck, I approached the couple now sitting on the bench together. He greeted me with a "Good morning", and I waved and returned the greeting as their dog moved over to my boot for the expected scratching behind the ears.

"You did quite well this morning" he observed. "It's been a few weeks since we've even seen a fisherman here in the morning. It was nice to watch."

"I had the lake to myself" I acknowledged, as I looked around once more. "And the fish cooperated to do the rest."

"Maybe they were just tired of waiting?" he said with a wink and a small grin.

One Small Trout

I laughed, but had to agree. "You're probably right. They did seem more than willing." And with that we exchanges pleasantries in hopes of a good day coming and parted ways. Back at the truck de-rigging, I had a strong feeling the gentleman was right. I think we were both tired of waiting.

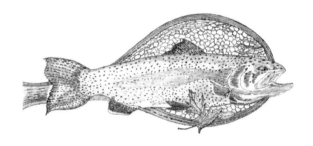

<u>Jersey Damsel</u>

The Jersey Damsel is a local pattern of mine that truly performs around small bass and bluegill waters. Tied to use on a dropper behind a bassbug, it has become an excellent stand-alone pattern as well when fished on a short leader with a floating line. This is one pattern that never lets you down.

<u>Jersey Damsel Recipe</u>

Hook: Standard Nymph Hook #10 2X Long

Thread: 6/0 Black Uni-Thread

Tail & Abdomen: 3 Strands Olive Ostrich Herl

Rib: Blue Medium Ultra Wire

WingCase: Wild Turkey Tail

Eyes: Medium Plastic Barbells

Thorax: Peacock Ice Dub

One Small Trout

Tying Instructions

1- Start thread and tie in barbell eyes 2 eye-lengths behind the eye of the hook.

2- Tie in ultra-wire behind the eyes and wrap back to the point of the barb.

3- Tie in 3 strands of ostrich herl at the barb leaving a shank-length tail. Folding the herl back along the wire.

4- Tie in the turkey tail wing-case behind the eyes and then pull them forward over the eyes and out of the way.

5- Palmer the ostrich her forward to the wing-case.

6- Counter wrap wire forward to the eye of the hook, pulling the wing-case back on the last wrap and securing in place with the wire. Tie off the wire.

7- Dub ice dub thorax crossing between the eyes and up to the eye of the hook.

8- Pull the wing-case forward and secure. Whip finish.

9- Coat wing-case with 2 coats of Head cement.

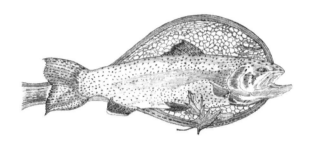

One Small Trout

Of Ants and Men

I had fished most of the pre-sun morning working my way downstream to the bridge, on a creek that my partner and I had fished a number of times before. Our agreement was I would walk the trail upstream and he would walk downstream, where we would then work our way towards the bridge in the middle and meet to compare notes. So far for my efforts I had been able to pull two small browns very early, with a subtle micro-caddis pattern in size 20 tied with a wood duck down-wing. Yet since those couple fish it had been nothing but inspections and rejections or the outright ignoring of my drifts.

I came around the last bend to the pool just above the bridge and noted my buddy, intent on changing flies. The tell-tale lowered head, rod under the arm and motionless appearance a dead give-a-way. I chuckled to myself as I enjoyed the view, having been in much of that same pose for most of the morning while trying to figure out just what these fish were expecting me to give them for breakfast. How could a creature with a brain the size of a pea be so stubborn I thought? Seconds later there I was again, gazing into my box in the very same pose. I had tried everything in the box already....except an ant pattern. "Can't hurt", I thought to myself, choosing a size 20 fur ant. It was your classic ant pattern with the dubbed body and small center hackle for legs. After cursing at my 7x fluorocarbon tippet for being nearly invisible in the bright sunlight, I finally managed to pierce the microscopic hook eye, tie the knot and apply floatant to the tippet. With my first cast I saw the little morsel of terrestrial offering leave its ring at the head of the pool. I tried to follow the route of the fly, but it was instantly in the film and invisible to my eye. My mind switched to a broader view of the surface hoping to see the swirl of a take in the film. I was not to be let down, however it did take place about 4 feet further downstream than I had guessed my fly to be. A lift of the rod and I was connected to another fish of 9 inches long as it began the electric dance of a stream-bred fish adorned with all its brilliant colors. I looked up after releasing the fish just as my buddy was playing a fish of his own to hand. Taking a moment to watch his victory take place as well, I reeled in and headed in his direction as he released the fish into the current and looked up.

Reaching his side we exchanged notes. He had done one fish better than I had throughout the morning. However, just as with my morning, they all came early and on dries. I looked at his hook keeper and laughed out loud. "How long were you fishing the ant?"

He shrugged as his eyes went to my rod as well, "Just changed to it here. You too?"

"Yep, I just decided to try it at the bridge. One cast and one fish for my efforts." I replied.

"Same here!" he laughed. "One cast, one fish."

We both backed off to the bank and took a seat on a couple of boulders to compare boxes and watch the water. Not really expecting to see any activity, since we doubted an ant hatch would come off any time soon, but it was an excuse to rest the legs. As far as ants go, our patterns were similar in size and color only. Most all of his patterns were chunky pieces of foam, orange yarn tied on top and plenty of glue and epoxy to be found. Mine on the other hand were primarily hackle-legged, built with dubbing and a bit of CDC thrown in on occasion. Both boxes were polar opposites for sure, yet we both have very similar success with our individual patterns. A fact that doesn't really allow either of us to lay claim to any superiority, but we still insist on doing so. He likes to chide me on being a hopeless romantic on the bench, and I accuse him of quitting fly tying for his new hobby of craft making with superglue and foam. When he catches a fish it's a new-age trout that wouldn't know a hopper from a cigarette butt, and when I hook-up the fish was probably blinded by a heron and can't tell the difference between an ant and a piece of pocket lint. It's the type of good natured banter that keeps us both happy and also helps to keep other fisherman on the water at a distance. It's a win-win in our book.

The differences pretty much stop there though. Our fishing styles mirror each other aside from the manner in which we both approach the tying bench. Although lately, with age and eyesight what it is, a little foam with an indicator spot would definitely help my cause. A fact that I will not offer up to him since it would lead to much grief on my behalf. A fact not missed judging by the abuse I took after he noticed a bottle of well-used Loctite on my bench last month. Some things are just better left to discovery over time; a very long time.

One Small Trout

Slipping out into the current of the crystal clear knee-deep water, I eased towards mid-stream in order to put myself within casting distance of a small pod of sipping trout along the far bank. Any disturbance would put them down for at least 20 minutes and to make things more difficult my 10 year old son was in tow as well. It was his first day with new hip-boots and his virgin sojourn into "fishing in the water" versus from the bank. His chatter punctuated by my insistence to "take it slow" was unending. However, much to my surprise it lacked the usual random nature of comments and questions that a parent grows accustomed to from a 10 year old boy. Instead, he was asking me how to step on rocks, commenting on how the cold water squeezed against his legs through the hip-boots, pointed out two Canada Geese that honked slowly as they flew overhead, and even once told me to slow-down because we were getting "awful close" as he put it.

Our goal was to get in position for me to make a cast, showing him the correct approach, and then he would get the rod. Stopping in range, I positioned him to my left to watch as he would be out of range of my right-handed casting. Glancing over at him he was bent over slightly at the waist with his hands on his thighs, intently observing the entire event as if he was a major league umpire. "No pressure Dad", I thought as I stripped out line for the cast. My first cast was on the mark and after a short drift brought a rolling rise but a swing-and-a-miss on the fly. On the short-rise he looked over at me in complete seriousness and declared, "You almost had him Dad. Give it to him again!" I chuckled to myself at his instruction and asked him if he wanted the rod now.

"No", was his reply, "I want to see you catch this guy" and with that he turned back to his umpire mode.

It took a couple more casts but eventually we got the rise we wanted along with a clean hook-up. The little fish came to hand nicely. It appeared to be a stream bred brown of about 5 inches long, and a beautifully colored example of what a trout can be. "We did it!" he exclaimed as I held the fish up for him to see.

One Small Trout

He intently looked the fish over, commenting on the orange spots along the flank, and the gold in its pectoral fins. He wet his hands to get a personal look at it, and then it was put back. But his comments lingered on at just how awesome that fish was. I again asked him if he wanted to fish more himself, but he answered no. Having worked most of the morning already on his casting he was done, intent now to simply wade along with me and flip the large flat rocks along the shore in search of crayfish. Not wanting to push things I let him go about his business. Having already shown promise in his casting, I figured his fishing lessons for the day were about complete.

We would catch one more fish of about the same size a bit further down the stream and then we packed it in for the day, heading back towards our friend at the cabin and a welcome fire. As any 10 year old, his energy was unstoppable. But the fire was a welcome relaxation point for Dad. Finally as the day drew to an end, he finally came over and opened his folding camp chair next to me for a few minutes. I asked him how he liked his day fly fishing. "It was awesome!" was his reply.

"I'm glad bud" I replied. "Too bad we didn't hammer them though. Maybe next time" I offered.

He looked up at me puzzled. "What do you mean?" he asked. "We caught fish".

"I know" I acknowledged, "But maybe next time we'll catch better fish."

He never even blinked with his response, and while still staring straight into the fire answered "Did you SEE those fish Dad? They were beautiful. Do the colors get better when they get bigger?"

I just stared at him as he watched the fire. "No Bud, not really" I answered.

He looked up at me and with the honest eyes of a 10 year old child, gave a small shrug and replied, "It don't really matter then does it?"

I was speechless for a minute, unable to do anything but smile. I was just looking at him as he looked back at me expecting an answer to confirm his thoughts. "Nope, is sure doesn't buddy." I answered. "You are right."

He pondered my answer for a moment, and then with what looked like the wisdom of an age-old fisherman of many years, turned and nodded to himself as he looked back into the fire as if to say, "Just as I thought."

I had just been reminded by a 10 year old boy just why it is that I am drawn to trout waters. It can be found in the beauty of the places in which they haunt, and in the moment of bringing a fish to hand. It's a place

One Small Trout

of near perfection, where some of life's most important lessons can be learned from a 10 year old boy and one small trout.

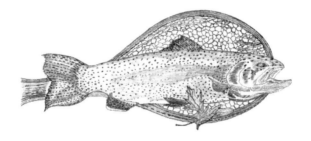

Little Olive Wet

This pattern is my first choice for the Fall Olives. I fish it in wet fly fashion with the last 6" of tippet greased heavy to keep the pattern in or near the film.

<u>Little Olive Wet Recipe</u>

Hook: Standard 2x Heavy Scud #14-18

Thread: Olive Dun Uni-thread 6/0

Abdomen: Olive Biot

Thorax: Olive Ice-Dub

Wing: Lemon Barred Wood Duck

Hackle: Silver Badger Brahma hen

One Small Trout

<u>Tying Instructions</u>

1- Start thread and wrap an form an even thread base to the barb of the hook

2- Tie in Biot and move thread forward to a point two eye-lengths behind the eye.

3- Tie in lemon wood duck with tips extending just past the bend of the hook.

4- Dub a slight thorax with ice-dub.

5- Tie in hen hackle and make two full turns.

6- Build head slightly back into the hackle and whip finish.

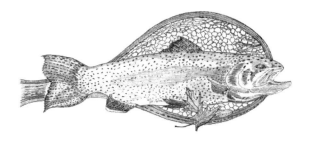

The Flow

The cool Pennsylvania limestone water was refreshing as it swept over a table of rock upstream of my position, rolling over itself in the head of the pool and stubbornly giving way to my waderless legs. For as long as I could remember, where I stood had always been a gravel bar during the last week of June. This year however, I stood in 12 inches of grass matted down by knee-deep current as I dredged a tandem nymph setup to trout in which I could see but, for whatever reason, could not catch. The stream was clear but high, with more rain forecast later in the day. Again nature would add to the trickle of life in which I stood, and in the end its water would reach the Susquehanna River where it would in turn nourish the Chesapeake. Pausing between casts I reached down and scooped up a handful of water, letting it trickle back to the stream through my fingers, watching as the breadth of the stream moved downstream, seemingly gone forever in the endless flow of water. Within the flow, were small pools, rock formed eddies and countless swirls and whirlpools caused by unseen forces below the water's surface. One thing above all stood out from the scene before me; it did not stop. It was perpetual. Though it may slow or gain in tempo, or the backdrop may become altered due to forces of nature, it did not stop. Like time, the water in which we encounter or enjoy in that moment is gone in an instant, never to be repeated in exactly the same manner again. We may enjoy another bit of water very similar to the one in past memory, but it will still be different in some way.

Turning back to the run before me I was clouded by these thoughts, which did not help my calamity caused by fish who would not take my flies. I had fished this run countless times in the past, and whenever they were flashing heavy with no sign of a hatch I would fish this same tandem with success. They always took one of the two flies presented, a size14 bead-head Squirrels Nest above a size18 Hares Ear. Today however, it was not to be. Also, gone were the two sweepers that had been just upstream of the bridge, which always kept the pool below the bridge stable. They had been

One Small Trout

repositioned downstream of the pool perpendicular with the bank by last year's storms. The affect was a leveling of the old pool, which was now bare river stone scrubbed free of the debris formed by the longtime pool. An alteration that was probably good for the ecosystem of the stream as a whole, but not something that was helping me at the moment. The hatch cycle of the pool was gone. And likewise, so were my effective fishing techniques. I would have to change. Stubbornly I blamed the stream, and looked to my fly boxes.

I decided to go with a small size 12 black Wooly Bugger, above a size 18 Pheasant Tail Nymph. Two casts into the change I was hooked into a nice fat rainbow and life was once again as it should be. At least it was from my perspective anyway. I moved downstream slightly after a few fish and caught a handful more as the change in flies proved productive. The fish however were smaller than many I had spotted in the steam. I decided to start again from the bridge abutments, and tied on a size 10 Northwest Jack streamer. Maybe this steady run with its submerged rocks would prove better streamer water. Halfway down the run I got my answer as a fat 18 inch Brown slammed my fly. Taking me to the far bank and down to the tail-out of the old pool, it pounded my little 4 weight as I fought to protect the 6x fluorocarbon tippet that I had forgotten to upgrade in my haste. Without a net for the day, I found myself kneeling in the shallows as I cradled the fish to remove the fly. It was beautiful, with undamaged fins and the coloration of a stream bred fish. I released it strong and watched as it headed straight back to the fast mid-current where I had hooked it. The water had changed.

Kneeling in a foot of water and seated back on the heels of my wading boots, the smooth rocks of the stream bottom were hard, but not unbearably uncomfortable on my knees. I took a few moments to look around. To a new observer things would seem perfectly normal for any stream. Yet to me, so much had changed. Had it not been for the bridge and cabins that still stood within view, this stretch of water could just as soon be in Montana. Gone was the stretch of water I knew, and likewise obviously gone were the hatches I knew as well. Would it return? Probably so, but there were no guarantees that it would ever return to the water I had grown up with. Like the waters flow, it could never again be exactly what it had been. It may return back to a semblance of what one remembered, but it could never again be exactly the same. That was simply not the course of nature. And would we really want it to? It was certainly not ruined, it was simply different yet perfect still in its own way. The water still moved perpetually over the same rock. It still hit those visible and hidden obstructions as it swirled along its course bending and molding to the surroundings it encountered. For fishermen, the flow of water shouts

One Small Trout

out to us in a voice that we cannot afford to let fall on deaf ears. Reminding us that holding too tightly to how things are, can blind us to the beauty of what things will be.

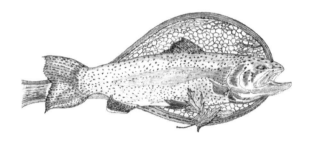

Fishing for Answers

Standing at streams edge I paused to check out the fledgling Robin that caught my eye as it lay among the wild mint. It was dead, but not stiff as of yet, so I scanned the tree above for the expected nest it would have either left or been dislodged from. There it was, about 10 feet up on the limb of a black birch tree. From my position the sounds of faint chirps came to my ear. What had caused the young birds life to be extinguished so early? Obviously I could not tell if it had an internal ailment, but it was an otherwise healthy looking specimen. By all accounts not more than a few moments ago the bird had been within that nest, chirping with the rest of them. Yet now, its life was gone and would live on only through the elements as nature would surely reclaim its body. Had it been sick and pushed out by the mother or its hungry siblings? Had it simply been impetuous in its youth and left too early and thus met an untimely death? Or had it been a victim of a predatory animal or bird that caused it to fall to its demise, and I was simply in the way at the moment? Looking around, I saw no other waiting critter, and the normal cadence of small chirps told me that all was well in their current world. Understanding that I would never really know what exactly had transpired I accepted the situation and moved on down the bank and into the water to address a pool where I was looking to test a new streamer.

The furnace hackled streamer was a new pattern I had envisioned during the winter two years earlier. It had done very well for me in its original state. However, I had made a few small changes to it this season, adding a longer red buck-tail throat, and replacing the silver rib with a rib of gold tinsel. The result, I felt, was a result of reflection after watching a small school of minnows converge on a piece of sandwich bread I had dropped in the water during a lunch stop the past summer. Watching them feed in competition I couldn't help but think the flash had more of a gold glint to it from my view, and the occasional red flare of the gills was unmistakable. So there I was, at the bench a day or so ago, tweaking an already proven pattern on a hunch. And likewise, the pool to test it on would be the same pool where I had watched those minnows feed.

One Small Trout

I had recalled my thoughts on the pattern while I was browsing a website and came across the patterns of a friend and acquaintance that had passed away a little over a year ago. I had traded patterns with him for years over the Internet and he had possessed an unbelievable talent for Rangeley Style streamers. They were a style I had seldom tied, yet over the years I had developed an appreciation for them as well. This was as much a testament to his friendship as well as his skill, since we had never actually had the opportunity to meet face-to-face. As it was, even without a mutual path in life to share, we had struck up a friendship through fly tying only. It was with surprise however that I learned of his illness and then shortly after, his untimely death at a far too early age. Why was it, I wondered, that I was now standing here in clear water contemplating a day on the water, yet life did not find it necessary for him to continue on? Not having knowledge of his personal life or health, I realized that I was as much in the dark with my friend as I was with the small bird that lay silently on the bank behind me. There were some things that would inevitably go unanswered, and just maybe that was how things are meant to be. Yet questions of fairness and the cruelty of nature and life have a way of creeping in on person. I had experienced my share of life threatening illness and situations over the years, yet here I was. So many others, including my parents had left this world sooner than they should have. Memories of those gone flooded in as I stood in the cold spring water. Was it by design? Or was it simply dumb luck? Was there a purpose for all of it, or do we all simply stroll through life experiencing whatever hits us, until it is our time as well? All of this and much more rumbled through my mind as I slowly worked the pool in front of me.

I was working the pool from its tail to the head, mainly due to the vegetation and not for any conscious thought of how to best fish the water. To cover the water in any logical manner, there really was only one way to go about things. I needed to strip a few more feet of line for my next cast in order to reach a small eddy along the far bank. A little extra effort and I smiled as the fly landed perfectly and my line was quickly caught up in the current. On the third strip of line everything went suddenly tight and I strip-set to a heavy fish. I was quickly able to identify the fish as a heavy butter-colored brown and was treated to a dance that seemed almost rehearsed as he walked through every way possible to thrown the burdensome hook that was embedded in his jaw. However, in the end on this day I prevailed and was soon admiring a hefty 18 inch fish covered in leopard spotting with silver-gray halos around the larger of the spots. Along its jaw I spied the streamer, the red throat contrasting brightly along the gold in its jaw and the dark furnace hackle of the wing. I popped it loose and with a quick flip that caught me slightly off guard the fish was gone, leaving nothing

One Small Trout

behind but the memory in my mind that our meeting had ever taken place. The fly had done its job, maybe my enhancements had worked after all?

Rinsing the fly, I stepped upstream as I recovered my line and moved into position for my next cast. It sure was a beautiful fish, I thought to myself. Then it hit me. Maybe everything is tied together in ways in which we can no sooner predict than we could duplicate? Like the random lines in a dream catcher, where all in which we touch or experience comes back around in some shape or manner. Had I not fly fished and tied flies I would have never met my friend. Had we not become friends I probably would have never had the desire to tie Rangeley streamers. It was the memory of my friend that brought me to the bench and helped me to recall the enhancements that I had made to my pattern and in turn brought me back to this pool. And it was here that I would encounter that small unfortunate bird, whose untimely death would prompt me to ponder both my own existence and the memories of those passed. All of which culminated into a perfect day on the water, a beautiful fish and a recollection of many fond memories. Or I had found a dead bird, caught a nice fish and have some great memories. I've decided that I can live with either one.

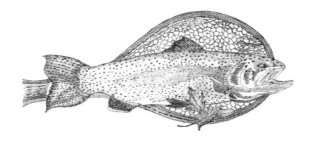

<u>Khaki Midge</u>

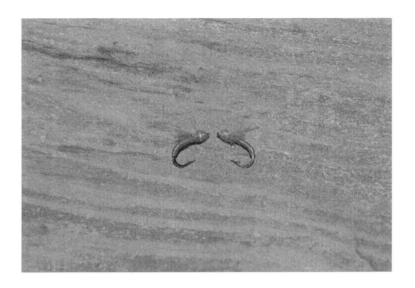

The Khaki Midge is the midge I encounter
more often than any other in Central
and Southern Pennsylvania. Tied in Size#20-#32, it can
make or break your winter midge fishing.

Khaki Midge Recipe

Hook: #20-#32 Caddis Emerger

Thread: Rusty-Dun Uni-Thread

Abdomen: Tying thread coated in Bug Bond

Thorax: Orvis Spectrablend Dark Dun

Wing: Dun CDC

One Small Trout

Tying Instructions

1- Start thread and wrap and form an even thread base to the barb of the hook, then wrap forward one eye length back from the eye of the hook forming a slightly tapered body.

2- Coat thread body with Bug Bond.

3- Dub a slight thorax.

4- Tie in CDC loosely with tips extended back over the shank, then fold the butts back over doubling the CDC and tie down securely.

5- Build a head and whip finish.

6- Lift CDC fibers and trim at a 45 degree angle towards the bend of the hook.

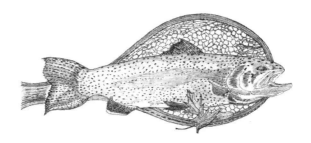

To Bead, Or Not To Bead

The indicator slipped slightly below the surface as my mind went through a moment of SPP, or "Stationary Piscatorial Panic". SPP is a common malady suffered by nymph/indicator fishermen. Even for the most seasoned of fly fishermen, when we are focused on that little strike indicator our senses seem to revert back to those of a high-strung 12 year old running on Little Debbie cakes and Coke. I've discussed it with many of my buddies and I am convinced the Fishing Gods are actually playing a cruel joke on us. I think it's punishment for renaming a "bobber" a "strike indicator" so that our fly fishing sensitivities will not be so disrupted as to require secret sessions of hanging out in well-known fly shops in order to make ourselves feel better again. It's their way of saying, "If you're going to fish with a bobber, deep down you cannot hide." Let's face it, "Trapped air technology!" Simply renaming how a standard plastic red-and-white bobber works, does NOT change the fact that it still remains a bobber. Nevertheless, like many of my fly fishing brethren there I was, double-clutching as my "indicator" slipped once again below the surface. Strike or bottom bounce? This time I won and with a lift of the rod a fine specimen of what this Pennsylvania limestone stream had to offer began its dance of protest at the intrusion of my hook. It came to hand after a nice little fight and staring back at me from the jaw of a fat little 12 inch brown trout was a size 14 bead-headed caddis pupae. It had been an easy guess having watched a haze of little tan caddis coming off the water, while seeing no rises above the constant flashing of bottom-feeding trout.

It was the sixth or seventh trout on that fly and it was taking a beating. So, deciding to swap out for a fresh fly, I sat staring at my patterns. I was most certainly going with another of the same pattern, but what caught my eye was the fact that virtually all of my patterns wore the helmet of a bead. When had that theme taken root? I seemed to recall not too long ago, that the reverse was the norm in my fly boxes. I always seemed to do much better with an impressionistic weighted non-bead-head fly pattern in the past. Having often joked among friends that I had never caught a single trout on the venerable bead-headed Pheasant

One Small Trout

Tail, or the Copper John, two of the most commonly fished bead-head patterns. And though neither of those two patterns were still in my box for that very same reason, in their place was row after row of very similar bead-head patterns. But again, what was it that caused the change? Was it that I had finally learned how to properly fish them? It seemed to me that I still fished in pretty much the exact same manner. Was it the addition of the thing-a-ma-jiggy that I still refuse to call a bobber currently looped onto my leader that did it? I doubt it, since before they were in my vest they were duplicated by yarn and foam indicators. So, no real change there either. But what "had" changed? The only thing that had really changed over recent years was the lack of using additional split-shot on my tippet these days. Thinking about it as I stood tying my new and un-chewed nymph on, it seemed that the only real change was going from brass beads to tungsten beads in my fly tying. I had found that the additional weight was generally all I needed when fishing bead-head nymphs now. But could that one thing have changed my style of fishing so dramatically?

I have to acknowledge in self-examination that I am very reluctant to change, and confidence in a fly is something that my lack of patience seldom lends support to. As a result, early experiences tend to stick with me for a while in the realm of fly selection. But that would only explain the lack of a few revered fly patterns from staking claims within my boxes. It did little to answer for the row-upon-row of bead-head flies that currently filled them. All of which these days were in fact tied with tungsten beads. Was it as simple as a tad-bit more weight on the fly, allowing me within my nymphing skills to skip the addition of split-shot on the leader? A change which may have led me to success and confidence in a particular bead-head pattern, and over time causing a wholesale migration back to my tying bench and the materials that I both buy and tie with. The only other culprit for the change could be the increased use of the item we refer to as the "strike indicator". But to accept that as the reason for change would further complicate the entire universe relative to fly fishing and our separation from the lowly bobber and its associated accoutrements.

These are the things that go through our minds or at least my mind when on the water. My grip on sanity however is maintained only by convincing myself that the rest of the fly fishing community thinks as I do. Please allow me to enjoy my moment. Most times these thoughts occur during the doldrums of prospecting on auto-pilot in hopes of strikes, but they can and often do take place during moments of perceived clarity even while playing and releasing fish. That being said, I have obviously made the transition to bead-heads. What I do with that new-found bit of piscatorial wisdom is yet to be seen.

The Fly or the Rise

In the world of fly tying an inevitable discussion is bound to rear its head from time-to-time. The discussion is much like that of the "chicken and the egg" question, but in piscatorial pursuits includes the "Fly and the rise". Or rather which came first, the pattern or the rise requiring the pattern? Sit around a campfire and if my experiences are the norm, you will hear a consensus that most patterns are tied to catch more fishermen than fish. I tend to agree, especially when considering the entire spectrum of patterns tied over the years. But what happens if the selection is narrowed down to those patterns that we keep over the long-term? Those tried-and-true patterns that just plain catch fish for whatever reason. Now, as a fly tyer I will be the first to admit when at the bench, artistic license often comes into play, which can in turn create some exaggerated and off-the-wall patterns. And as luck would have it, those "artistically inspired" creations at times turn out to be great producers of fish. Though I will admit when alone in a room with just myself listening, that far too often they produce nothing and end up in my throw-away bin. Beautiful they are, but useful they prove not.

Now for some tying styles mind you, such as the Atlantic salmon patterns, artistic flare is the defining part of each pattern. Over the years they have become as much a coat-of-arms to a particular tyer then anything remotely associated with that of catching fish. Yet endure they do, and we love them for it. However, trout fishermen pride themselves at knowing their quarry so well, and studying the hatches in which they feed on to the umpteenth degree, that you would think all patterns for trout would come first-and-foremost from the "rise". We all know the scene. Fish are rising all around you but refusing every fly in your box. Then, out of the corner of your eye you see a fluttering bug and catch it, revealing a previously unnoticed shade to a local pattern. It's that twinkling of an eye when experience meets knowledge, and experienced hands turn towards the bobbin and vise to produce a bit of wisdom on a hook. Certainly that must be the case the majority of the time in the birth of trout patterns. And then one steps into a fly shop and peers into the bins at

One Small Trout

a Turk's Tarantula, a Golden Retriever, a Parmachene Belle or even the venerable Royal Wulff. It's then that he finds himself scratching his head and wondering just what rise did any of those tyers witness that inspired those patterns. I am certain if asked, each pattern has a logical explanation as far as the creator is concerned. But in the end, I would bet more artistic hunch and possibly a bit of boredom came into play at some point. Neither of which is a bad thing mind you when at the bench. Besides, the end results for each of those aforementioned patterns speak volumes for themselves over the course of many years. Never-the-less, our reality is that there are just as many effective patterns that were born due to wisdom and imagination at the vise verses that which is gathered on the water.

However, I think we also are now living in a golden age of change within the fly tying community. There are additional forces in play over recent years that are driving the new patterns in which we find in those pro-shop bins each spring. Technology and innovation within today's markets are producing annual crops of new materials in which the tyer has to choose from. And each spring we are seeing revised patterns and tying techniques developed around a newly created material. We are seeing face-lifts to decades-old patterns that in turn are generating huge reports from the water. These new materials and techniques, one would think, would further muddy the water surrounding the original question, or does it? I think it actually bridges the gap in many ways between knowledge and artistic imagination, where a person with knowledge of the water who also possesses the imagination at the vise actually views each hatch and pattern in a new light, cast by the additional materials and techniques at hand. It's at this place in time where a new fly tying "trinity" is formed of Entomology knowledge, skill at the vise and the artistic vision of all the materials at hand. OR it could just be a case of a Piscatorial Nimrod such as myself, sitting at his bench while looking at a new material in his hand and saying, "Cool, this stuff is shiny!" Then proceeding to mutate every pattern in which he thinks it could possibly work, in the hopes of finding that next great pattern.

RuffChuck

The RuffChuck gets its name from the materials in which it was tied. It is a true cross-over pattern, lending itself to trout and warm-water equally as well. Bottom-bounced or drifting under an indicator, this pattern produces.

R.E. Long

RuffChuck Recipe

Hook: #6 Mustad C67S

Thread: 3/0 Red Uni-thread

Eye: Tungsten Dumbell

Tail: Ruffed Grouse Marabou

Body: Amber Ice-Dub

Wing: Woodchuck guard-hairs

One Small Trout

Tying Instructions

1- Build a thread base in the thorax portion of the shank and tie in the barbell eyes. Secure firmly.

2- Tie in Ruffed grouse Marabou with the tips extending 1 ½ shank lengths beyond the bend of the hook.

3- Dub the abdomen up to a point one eye length back from the eye of the hook.

4- Turn the fly over and tie in the Woodchuck hair with the tips even with the tips of the marabou. Split them with the point of the hook.

5- Build a substantial tapered head, whip finish and coat with 2 coats of head cement.

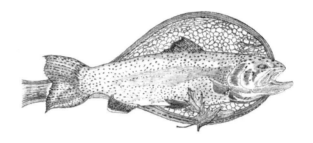

Comfort Fly

Pausing to look over the stream I took a seat on a large maple sweeper that had found the dry gravel its seasonal resting place. Perpendicular to the waters course, it was as if nature had envisioned a need for a bench overlooking the long glide in front of me and simply placed the woeful tree in the center as a gift to fishermen. I had begun my morning at daybreak in order to escape the worst of the mid-August heat. The fish however, had only partially cooperated with my efforts. They initially seemed agreeable to rising steadily all morning which had me optimistic, yet they had refused to eat any of my offerings which resulted in a torment that most of us know all too well. It was now 10 am, and the sun which was beginning to find a direct path to the creek had the ball cap I was wearing thoroughly saturated in sweat. I pulled my vest off and hung it on the remnants of a broken branch in order to get to the back pocket and the water bottle that was hopefully at least still slightly cooler than body temperature.

The pool before me was on a long sweeping bend that wrapped around the tree I was perched upon, before dropping into a huge plunge pool that tailed out into a boulder field. I had hoped to find the remnants of a Trico hatch here to plant myself over until the heat got to be too much, but it didn't look to be the case today. I had only been able to bring one fish to hand all morning. A fat rainbow of 15-16 inches that had decided it liked a size 22 Griffith's Gnat better than the grey midges that were the object of most of its attention up until that point. Aside from that, the morning had been filled with refusals and outright piscatorial abstinence.

As I sat enjoying the lukewarm, but at least wet bottle of water, I was finding no rise-forms. Thinking I could switch to a nymph and dredge the pool top-to-bottom, I scrutinized my box. Being a stubborn creature by nature I was hoping to find a pattern and stick with it on this final pool of the morning. My mind however, while it knew the water screamed "nymph", kept migrating back to a dry caddis pattern. The Penn's Grannom pattern is one of my own that over the years has grown to be a favorite when confidence is low. I think we all have at least one of them. It's that pattern that seems to more-often-than-not save an otherwise fishless day. And regardless of whether it's time on the water, or sheer happenstance that brings it success, each time a fish rises to it the position within your psyche is more deeply ingrained. That fly for me is the PG. It's a fairly basic and simple to tie pattern, and a local variation of the age-old Fluttering Caddis. Tied with an olive-brown dubbed abdomen and thorax, it sports a natural CDC under-wing, a light elk down-wing and Golden badger hackle. In size #14-18 it's a near perfect match to a large number of the caddis hatches I encounter locally, and one that the fish seem to prefer. So, once again I found myself re-building my tippet and tying on a size 16 Penn's Grannom, gathering up my gear and heading up to the head of the pool. My goals were to pound every inch of the run and presumably convince the finicky fish of the day to leave their lies in pursuit of my caddis fly.

I began as if fishing over a steelhead run, hitting the near eddy first, then a couple passes through the heart of the run, and ending on a drift or too along the far bank. Then a few steps downstream and repeat the process. On my third cast while in the heart of the run it happened. A 14 inch brown hammered the fly with no hesitation and instantly I knew the PG was at it again. It was as if there was a caddis hatch coming off yet not another bug or rise was to be seen, but fish were rising even from deep water to take the fly. Some wanted it skittered, some dead-drift, and some hammered the pattern as it drowned toward the end of the drift. It seemed that no matter what I did the fish keyed on the pattern, and the end of the run found me happy and smiling. The heat of the sun was gone from my mind and I had brought to hand more than a dozen fish in the past hour, after an otherwise fishless morning.

I stood in the tail-out of the pool inspecting my tattered fly and wondering just what it is that makes it work. Was it an attribute within the pattern? Or was it the confidence it gives me when fishing it? Or should I even care? Like many folks speak of a number of patterns that have been handed down over the years as being their go-to fly, this particular pattern had obviously become mine. It had now entered that much heralded category of banana splits, Pittsburgh-rare steak with Guinness, and scrapple with eggs most anytime. It was now officially my "Comfort Fly".

Glurp Goes the Cricket

It began like any other spring day does; cool in the morning with birds chirping a serenade through your bedroom window. The kind of wakeup that makes you wish all mornings were exactly like this one. So, in a good mood right off the get-go I sat at the kitchen table with my first cup of black coffee and watched the sun rise. While sitting there, I flipped through my cellphone to check the forecast for the day, and was surprised to see a high of 75 degrees with no wind. Instantly my mind went to bluegills. I tend to not bother with panfish on the fly until I see a good solid warming trend, and this could just be the beginnings of the first of the year. The rest of the morning crawled by as I worked distracted on a few honey-do's, but all the while watching that thermometer creep up. Wrapping up the last one that I felt could be done before lunch time; I headed for my gear and grabbed my Far-and-Fine for no other reason but that it had not been used since winter. I made sure there was a new leader attached. It just felt right and a 5 weight would be all I needed on this trip. I quickly went through my fly box and grabbed a half dozen new-and-used Foam-Butt Caddis for the trip. Maybe a struggling cricket would do the trick on a warm spring day? I felt that I was soon to find out.

Wanting to eat quickly, I threw together a German Bologna sandwich and grabbed a cold beer from the fridge. Seconds later both were gone and I was searching for my wife. I nonchalantly brought up conversation in a casual manner, and then probably far too soon into working up to the announcement I proclaimed that I thought I would go fish a little bit since it was such a nice day out. My announcement was met with a smirk and a shaking of the head in amazement as she reminded me that she had already seen it coming and that she wondered why I hadn't gone earlier. A quick kiss on the cheek left me walking towards my gear and wondering just how I could have missed that opportunity. And how I had obviously just squandered what could have been the best morning of fly fishing in my life. But now I would never know! You would think at 50 years old I would be better at picking up on those things but obviously not. Note to self. Pay better attention!

One Small Trout

It took me another ½ hour to get my float tube and gear around, and by the time I was ready to go the temps were nearing 72 degrees. I made the short 2 mile trip to the local pond in short order, and once again went through the circus event of getting oneself into waders, fins and strapped into the tube. At first glance one would envision a very large 5 year old in a giant pool floatie. And on 2nd glance one would clearly see an over-fed grey haired man trying not to kill himself on land while wearing swim fins. The local gaggle of geese even waddled by and hissed at me. But I somehow feel that in goose language they were saying, "Get a load of this one Murray. Five pieces of bread says he falls. Watch this." I set myself adrift with little grace, and looking around I think all the young kids with their spinning rods felt they had just witnessed the launching of a freshly minted tuna boat. I quickly kicked myself away from them and headed backwards towards the shallow end and its lily pads. Having once been a kid myself, I would feel a tad bit safer far away from their spin-cast rods and Rapalas.

Turning to face the lilies, I began stripping line out. I was faced with a 50 yard half-moon line of pads which were the target of my intentions. Gaining enough line airborne I let the little foam and elk-hair cricket pattern touch the surface about 12 inches short of the plants. Two twitches later and with a "glurp", the fly disappeared and I was entertained by a palm-sized bluegill on the end of my line. I enjoyed the fight and then slid him up on my tube apron and released him to rise another day. Six casts later I was likewise releasing my 6th fish and smiling at my beaten and gnarled fly. "You're earning your pay today Glurp" I said to my fly out loud as I affectionately named it. Seconds later on the next cast it disappeared in another rise and the scene repeated itself. Forgotten were Sunday chores, the next day's work or the many trials of life. All that remained was the water, my fly rod and that little black cricket pattern. As I finned my tube along the pads catching fish after hungry fish I neared the far bank, where 2 boys stood fishing together. The younger of the two yelled out to me, "Hey mister, what are they biting on!?"

I turned my tube with a scissor kick and replied "Glurp".

"Thanks" the older one said with a wave. Then I heard him say to his buddy with a shove to the shoulder, "I TOLD you we should have gotten some of that Berkley Glurp at the bait shop!"

I was still laughing to myself as once again Glurp took another plunge into the swirl of a rise and the dance resumed. Yup, spring was here to stay.

Appleseed

The Appleseed is a personal pattern of mine and one that has served my box exceedingly well over the course of the past 8 years or so. During the Apple Caddis hatch this pattern turns those splashy rising fish into fish-in-hand.

Appleseed Recipe

Hook: #14 Scud

Thread: 6/0 Olive Uni-thread

Abdomen: Tan Micro-tubing over Olive Uni-thread

Thorax: Olive Ice-dub

Wing-case: Mottled Wild Turkey Tail

Hackle: Light Furnace Hen Neck

One Small Trout

<u>Tying Instructions</u>

1- Tie in thread and wrap back to the mid-way point of the bend.

2- Tie in micro-tubing.

3- Wrap back to the point of the thorax with the tying thread forming an even base.

4- Wrap micro-tubing forward over the tying thread to the point of the thorax and tie off.

5- Tie in the wing-case extended toward the bend of the hook.

6- Dub the thorax.

7- Tie in the hackle and wrap one full turn in wet fly fashion.

8- Sweep hackle fibers down into the position of the throat of the fly and secure.

9- Pull the wing-case over and whip finish.

10-Apply a light coat of Bug-Bond over the wing-case.

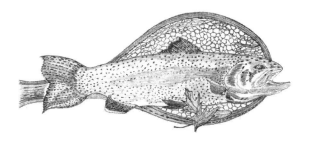

Swapping Flies

I have an old flat foamed SA fly box that is adorned with stickers, writing, and a strip of duct tape to help hold the latch closed. It's an endearing part of my tying ensemble and I cringe each time it gets placed into an envelope with the US Postal Service. The value of this box is small in monetary comparison, yet the worth is immeasurable to me personally. The little grey box has travelled the world on countless excursions holding flies from my bench while returning filled with that much and more, yet I have never accompanied it along its travels. The fly box I speak of is my Swap Box.

Within the online fly tying community there is a practice called a ""fly swap". One person will post the swap on a forum and function as the Swap Master, declaring what the guiding theme for the patterns tied will be. The theme is often guided by the time of year and the hatch that may coincide, or a particular style of tying such as Streamers, Nymphs, or Dry Flies. Many will be simply to tie your favorite fly, or your most productive pattern. One of my favorite themes is to have everybody tie their version of a classic pattern. I always enjoy seeing the returned flies reflecting how an individual tyer views or chooses to tie a given pattern. The regional and material choices are often very telling, and many times will cause me to take a hard look at my own version as well. Swaps are usually all inclusive, bringing in all-comers from experienced professional to novice tyers seeking to learn from the return patterns or compare where they are in their skill progression. I have found that regardless of the level of tyers involved, I am always able to glean either a technique or style that will affect my tying in some way as well.

Here's how it works. The Swap Master will announce a new Swap on a forum, and declare a theme. Let's say "Favorite Streamers" for example. He will also declare how many intended swappers he wants to handle and the tying deadline, or the latest date he will need to receive your flies. A dozen is about average, since too many can be burden for all to meet. If the swap is for 12 people, all swappers that sign on are agreeing to tie at least 11 flies in their given pattern and send them in a package that includes their box, along with a SASE for the swap master to return once all flies are received. They need not include a pattern counting themselves. A toe tag of a piece of paper is generally attached to each hook identifying the tyer and the name of the pattern. Once the swap master receives all of the patterns, he/she will sort one pattern from all tyers into each return box, minus one of their own. They are then mailed back in the included packaging. Often tyers will tie additional patterns or add trinkets as a gift to the swap master for their efforts as well. But nothing is expected from either side aside from the flies intended.

I have received a number of things through swaps that were unexpected and have since become items of attachment for my tying bench over the years. One of which is a custom bodkin inscribed by the maker that has been on my bench now for about 12 years. I still swap with that gentleman every year as well. I have lapel and hat pins tied as flies, Ornaments and decorative ties, as well as a few display salmon fly patterns that are framed. You never know what you will find when that package arrives. Swapping flies for me is akin to attending a tying conclave without actually seeing the other members face-to-face. Quite often you will get a fly tied with considerable talent, only to find out that it was tied by a youngster after completing his middle-school homework. It can leave you shaking your head in awe. There are a few patterns tied by well-known folks that are kept along with their toe-tags, and a few that have become standards in my own boxes as well.

I recently completed a swap that included folks from all over North America and the Far East. Many of whom I have swapped with before. Times like this are genuinely enjoyable because though I've not met any of them face-to-face, they are considered friends that I have known for many years. It is unavoidable that some tyers who I have come to know through swaps have passed over to the other side of the stream. Some of their flies are kept in a small tin that I keep in remembrance. Others are simply a good thought that crosses my mind each time I send a package downstream. It has become an integrated part of my fly tying life over the years that has built friendships and furthered my tying knowledge and skills. And so it is that I tape the little grey box shut once more for transport. Looking down at the front I notice the Classic Salmon fly swap sticker that was the cause of its first journey. Today, it is filled with small bluegill hair poppers that I spent much too long worrying over to send away. But I must. They are accompanied by 3 streamers for the swap master for his efforts. I wonder if those on the other end are the same as I, waiting for that package filled with new patterns to arrive? Is it their first swap? Or will my patterns be a welcome and familiar name to them? Hopefully in its journey my little grey box will be treated well.

The Plunge

As most fly fishermen know, spend any amount of time on the water and eventually you will take the plunge. Not the type of plunge as in going to bamboo rods, high-end gear or two-handed spey casting. I'm referring to the literal "plunge" where one's self gets fully immersed in the waters we wade. Some get that initiation out of the way as a novice just learning to wade. In this case you are lucky and have an excuse. You didn't know any better, "I'll never make that mistake again" often applies to this situation. Hence, you save face to a larger degree. But for others it often comes later in our fly fishing journey. When experience leads to confidence, confidence leads to complacency and complacency leads to total surprise and complete shock when the moment arises. These events are the ones talked about around campfires, tying enclaves and general gatherings. Wherever fishermen are found who were fortunate enough to have borne witness to the event in person. When the experienced wader does take the plunge, it is usually shadowed by the knowledge of what the inevitable outcome will almost certainly be even as it's happening. We understand this because we "know" better than to have made the initial mistake which kicked the entire event into motion to begin with. For the novice wader as the event unfolds, he/she is often herd muttering "What the!?" or some such other unidentified mumbled phrase in surprise. However, the experienced wader to a person will more often than not declare "OH S%!$" since he/she already knows. No surprise of the outcome involved once the mistake is made only the instant acceptance of reality.

My first plunge as an experienced wader took place on a very cold Washington State coastal river during the spring steelhead run. This is compounded by the fact that the water involved is spring glacial run-off, and that "spring" is a misnomer since the weather was 40 degrees and raining. I was fishing with a good friend Troy, and while attempting to turn around and head for shore in the thigh deep run that passed over the slick piece of table-rock upon which I stood the unfortunate event happened. Knowing full well that you never lift

One Small Trout

your downstream leg and turn "into" the current when in moving water, I did exactly that. As I lifted my downstream foot to turn the current caught the toe of my wading boot. The effect was to do an almost a perfect pirouette in 5 mm neoprene waters, thick hoodie, wool sweater and wading jacket. Then, with both arms outstretched and swinging a fly rod I slapped face-down into the water with a loud "POP". I came to my hands and knees gasping from the cold, and then stood as two things happened. First, my body screamed for help as the water which was very recently ice slowly migrated to nearly every place that skin existed. Secondly, Troy's laughter grew louder with every awkward step that I took towards the bank. He had the right and the duty to honor my plunge in this fashion, since he was fortunate enough to have witnessed it in person. So I could only shiver and half-heartedly laugh along with him in proper steel-header etiquette. My take away from the event was not really what I had done wrong. I already knew not to do that prior to doing it. What I vividly recall thinking at the time, was that all those folks you read and hear about in those "polar bear society" events; they are all complete morons.

My second most memorable plunge came on the upper gorge of the Little Naches River in Eastern Washington while fishing the plunge holes with my buddy Darryl. We stood side by side on the rim of a 30 foot section of scree bank looking down into a likely hole below. We were both still looking down when I said, "I wonder if we can get down from here?" The instant I completed my question, the bank gave way under my feet and was suddenly sliding on my heels down the bank, miraculously keeping my balance as I surfed through ankle deep rock like Goofy in a Sunday morning Disney cartoon. I may even have used some of his hoots and hollers that we all know so well. But again, the foregone conclusion of what was about to happen was vividly painted in my mind as I rapidly approached the stone bench at the bottom, and when my feet hit that rock, my momentum was a force to be reckoned with. It instantly catapulted me out into that great looking pool with a splash as I curled up, bracing for impact. Standing up in the chest deep water, yet still holding my fly rod, Darryl's answer was loud and clear. "YES!" he answered, then headed for an easier route downstream while laughing hard enough to wake any Yeti still hiding in the Cascades.

The plunge happens to all of us eventually, though for some sooner or more often than others, but in the end, it's coming. I have a good friend that falls more than most. I'm not sure whether it's a result of aggressive wading or clumsiness though, since he does catch a lot of fish along the way. Spend a lot of time on the water and fate will rear its ugly head eventually and bring you closer to the water than intended. One must accept and embrace the inevitable. As long as no

One Small Trout

misfortune or injury is involved, it is simply the price we pay for pursing trout in these beautiful but often very cold waters. And remember, when it does happen witnesses are allowed to laugh. It's their piscatorial right as fishermen to relish in your plunge, and then retell the events of the account at every chance.

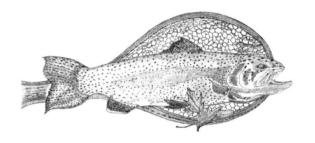

<u>Summer Caddis</u>

The Summer Caddis was named as it copies a group of
mid-summer caddis that hatch along many
of Pennsylvania's waters. Once the summer heats up
these larger lumbering caddis appear and are a daily
staple for surface feeding. This pattern is a steady
producer and one of my favorite prospecting patterns
when no real surface activity is apparent.

Summer Caddis Recipe

Hook: #12 Standard Dry

Thread: Brown Uni-thread

Abdomen: Gold Turkey Biot

Wing: 2 Natural CDC Puffs

Thorax: Peacock Herl

Hackle: Golden Badger

One Small Trout

<u>Tying Instructions</u>

1- Tie in the thread and form an even base back to the barb of the hook.

2- Tie in the Turkey Biot tip-first at the barb and bring the thread forward to the thorax.

3- Apply a light coat of head cement to the top of the thread base and wrap the biot forward, tying off and clipping the butts at the thorax.

4- Tie in both CDC feathers in delta fashion forming the wing.

5- Tie in the hackle.

6- Tie in the peacock herl and palmer forward to the eye of the hook.

7- Wrap the hackle forward over the peacock herl and whip finish.

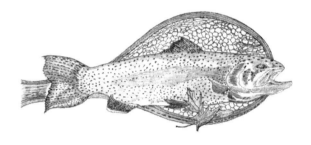

Passing of Waters

Sitting on a large freestone boulder I looked out over the pool in front of me and worked my left hand in hopes of a bit of control returning to it. The tremor was worse today, and although it wasn't keeping me off the water, it was certainly hampering me in my efforts. I needed to tie on a size 18 Blue-winged Olive emerger, and the effort had become fruitless after about 15 minutes of frustrating attempts. SO, rather than ruin my entire morning in a rage of stubbornness that I was obviously born predisposed to, I chose instead to take a seat. The boulder looked out of place, a much more course stone than any of the smaller river stones surrounding it. I wondered just where its journey had begun. From what deposit upstream of its current position did the waters dislodge it? Sitting awkwardly in the middle of a gravel bar certainly was not the starting point nor would the current position be its last. Though it may gather moss for a period of time, my intuitions told me that eventually the storms would rage once more and the boulder would find its way just a tad bit further downstream. Like it or not, it was at the mercy of nature's cycles. I was however thankful for its existence none-the-less, and relaxed against the massive weight to ponder just what had landed me upon this solid perch.

At times in life a seemingly immovable object can be a blessing of safe harbor, such as this rock was now, or it can be a perceived obstacle one smashes himself against in futility. Wasting effort and self, striving toward a conclusion that is in itself unattainable. That is a position where I had often found myself in the past. And although wisdom acquired in loss is often so clear in hindsight, I did in fact break myself in many ways striving for the unattainable. Thankfully, with that hard-earned wisdom there dwells an acceptance. Not the destructive acceptance of failure or a lesser station in personal being. But the acceptance of knowing when something is unwinnable. And once that point is reached, you can finally step back and see just how many previously unseen jewels are staring you square in the face.

One Small Trout

For many years I had always fished hard; covering a lot of water and priding myself in spotting the best lies, and finding the fish through persistence. Often fishing water successfully only to sit back later and not be able to recall clearly a single step along the way. It was the aggression of youth seasoned with a little bit of knowledge and a dash of that unstoppable drive to win. Unfortunately, along with that unstoppable drive, come the highest of highs when victorious, shaded by the lowest of lows whenever failure reared its ugly head. The price of youth is high, and when the collector comes around one can be humbled to the core. Thus was the case as I sat myself on that rock. In my youth I had earned my beret, the respect of many and most importantly the love of my family. Failure was never an option. And the word "Quit" was stricken from the English language as I knew it. Yet as I sat looking at my hand, I knew in my heart-of-hearts that this battle was unwinnable. When suddenly, a bit of hard-earned wisdom stepped forward and slapped me in the face. This was not a battle. This was life. It was the passing of waters over time and wherever the waters carry us there is a perfect view to be had. It may not be the view you had expected, but it is still perfect. So I sat; with my fly box now stowed I watched the fish rise across the pool. They were indeed rising to Blue-winged Olives, so I had been correct in my initial assumptions. I watched a nose again break the surface rising up to take a fly as it struggled in desperation to take flight. The violence of death, often witnessed in nature, yet it was done so with the beauty of a ballet, that was seemingly played out at that very moment for my eyes only. I saw the swallows working overhead as the sky blossomed into a million colors of a spring sunset colliding with the night air. Taking it all in I reveled in the display as all thoughts of my tremors and the ailments of age faded. When I finally looked around me, the light was fading and the hatch had diminished. A slight mist was forming over the tail-out of the pool as the cooling of the night air met the still warmer waters. There were a few fish rising steadily in the glassed surface of the pool as I calmly tied on a size 14 Elk Hair Caddis and walked to the water's edge. The casting stroke came naturally as the double-tapered line presented a perfect cast a few feet in front of the lead fish. As the little blonde fly passed over where I believed the fish was holding he indeed complied, rising up and sipping in my offering. The rod danced and the heavily spotted brown fought doggedly as I slowly began to sense he was tiring. Kneeling in the shallow water of the tail-out I unhooked it and felt its life surge as it kicked from the palm of my hand. Standing, I placed the bend of my hook in the hook keeper as I noticed the tremors were gone for now. They had not stopped me from fishing. They had instead offered me a ringside seat to a wonderful display of nature, and then in its closing act had provided a fish willing to rise.

The Skillet

A few times a year I get a hankering for fish fried creek-side in cast iron. I am not sure just what it is that triggers it, but on this particular trip I knew it was the cool mornings and turning leaves that were my downfall. Sometimes I think it's my inner-fisherman that spawns the urge, after witnessing dozens of trout released throughout a season's time on the water. At some point it has just had enough and says, "My turn". So as with this occasion, I found myself gathering up my things in a small hunting daypack I have to spend a day fishing some and relaxing a bit more along a quiet stretch of water.

R.E. Long

The necessity for the excursion consists of the same few things each time. It's a ritual so-to-speak, which has been paired down to accommodate my tastes alone. A 10 inch cast iron skillet, a small metal spatula, a small plastic container of bacon drippings (about a spoonful from the previous breakfast), a small spice shaker (salt, pepper, paprika blend), a small 6-cup enamel coffee pot, my camp cup and my camp silverware set. Not a lot. I eat out of the skillet and my coffee is brewed from creek water.

Pulling in along the two-lane road in central PA, I gave myself enough room to clear my mirrors from timber and gas trucks and got my gear ready. From my entry point I knew I could cut through the woods about ¼ mile before intersecting with the upper reaches of one of my favorite streams. It's a popular stream down further near the bridges, but up here you seldom find a soul. It was a section I had found while bow hunting the state forest a number of years ago. This morning however would be for fly fishing, since I already had a fat 5-point in the freezer which ended my season for a time. The fall woods were ablaze in color as I moved from sections of pine, through beech stands, then over an oak covered ridge which dropped down into a hemlock flat which signaled the approach of the creek. Standing on the river rock bank along the water I looked out over the long glide that funneled out of a large pool just upstream. The two sections stretched for

One Small Trout

about 300 yards, and would be my home for the morning. I dropped my pack along the bank and rigged the Far-and-Fine with a size 12 Limestone and a size 16 Green Skittle on an 18 inch dropper. Then I chose to start up top and work my way back downstream to my gear.

On my second cast I was rewarded with a fat little native brookie of 9 inches. Its heart's desire was the Skittle and I admired the brilliant fall colors as it slid from my hand. I was hoping for two or three fish in the 10 inch range to satisfy my appetite. I worked the pool thoroughly catching several more fish and eventually bringing to hand a fat 12 inch brown. It was a nice start towards lunch. Then near the tail-out I was surprised as a large fish left the water and took with it the Limestone! In short order I was holding a rainbow just shy of 20 inches with a brilliant scarlet flank and spotting resembling that of a Spring Steelhead. It was quite a beautiful fish with the beginnings of a hook to its jaw beginning to show. A quick picture and the fish kicked out of my hand and back into the pool. Too big for the pan anyway, and too much of a memory to fry up, I would fish on for some of his smaller kin. I was not to be disappointed, as 3 more fish later another thick-backed 10 inch brown took the Skittle and I was done.

Moving back to my gear I de-rigged the rod, put my chest pack in the backpack then turned to gathering a bundle of firewood for my dinner. Nothing big mind you, since I wouldn't be there long, just enough to stoke the coffee and heat the skillet for my lunch. Cleaning the trout in the stream, I tossed the entrails back into the hemlocks as my contribution to the local raccoon population. Evidence of their visits was all over near the pool just upstream. I sat fussing with the fire to get it "just so" as I waited for the coffee to come to a boil. Once it was brewed I would start my fish. In no time at all it seemed the coffee was to the side and the fish were sizzling away. A dash of seasoning on both sides and the skin crisped in the bacon lard was the method which has been my favorite form of fish since childhood. I picked the bones clean as I watched what looked to be a slight Blue-winged Olive hatch coming off at the tail of the pool. I enjoyed a visit from a matched pair of wood duck for a few minutes that seemed none-too-worried about my fire. Then I sat enjoying my coffee, as I watched a mess of crows harass a great horned owl which seemed only to want a moment of respite away from their racket. "I feel your pain" I said out loud as I watched him in his plight. There's nothing worse than the world being on your back when all you want is a little bit of quiet. "You should try fly fishing" I chuckled to myself as I lifted my cup in a toast on his behalf.

Once my coffee was gone, I dumped and rinsed my pot, heated up a skillet full of hot water to wipe my pan clean, then doused my fire. My walk back to the

One Small Trout

truck was slow and quiet. No therapy in the world could replace the affect the morning had on my mental wellbeing, and even my fly fishing thoughts were cleansed and content. I was back. And all it took was a 10 inch cast iron skillet.

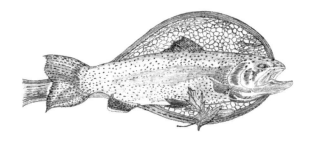

<u>Valley Caddis</u>

The Valley Caddis Nymph is one of my personal favorites. Tied originally for Valley Creek in Valley Forge PA, it began as a whim at the vise and ended up one of my best producing nymphs on most every water. Sometimes you tie a pattern with the best of hopes and it just spends time getting wet and enjoying the stream. The Valley Caddis spends most of its time drifting along and getting chewed on, which is a good thing as far as fly patterns go. Easy to tie and productive on the water pretty much sums this pattern up.

Valley Caddis Recipe

Hook: #12-16 Standard Scud/Caddis

Thread: Black 6/0 Uni-thread

Weight: 5-6 wraps of .015 lead wire

Rib: Medium Orvis Olive Body Glass

Shellback: Wild Turkey Tail Fibers

Abdomen: Natural Haretron

Legs: Lemon Wood Duck

Thorax: Natural Haretron

One Small Trout

Tying Instructions

1- Form a thread base and apply 5-6 turns of lead wire, beginning even with the point of the hook, forward to a point two eye-lengths behind the eye. Over wrap well with thread.

2- Tie in micro tubing behind the lead wraps and wrap back to a point mid-way into the bend of the hook.

3- Tie in turkey wing fibers behind the lead, and wrap back to the mid-way point of the bend of the hook.

4- Dub the abdomen up to the middle of the lead wraps.

5- Pull the turkey forward forming a shellback.

6- Wrap the micro tubing forward over the abdomen and tie off.

7- Pull the butt ends of the turkey back towards the bend of the hook and secure.

8- Tie in the Wood Duck fibers split evenly, extending the tips to the bend of the hook.

9- Dub a tapered thorax.

10- Pull the wing-case forward, splitting the wood duck evenly, and tie in behind the eye of the hook.

11- Whip finish an apply Bug Bond to the thorax portion of the wing-case.

Summer Bugs

Summer heat, deer hair and lily pads share one thing in common....Bugs. Deer hair ones, built for the jaws of hungry bass and the trials of being ripped through a lily pad jungle. They range from spectacular works of art in sizes built to entice ten pound bass and pike into a feeding frenzy; to plain colored variations tied small enough to bring a decent sized bluegill to the top. They are the soup-de-jour of summer. I have an affinity for them and have since a very young age. At 10years old my first fly rod came along with a handful of wet flies. Parmachene Belles, Cowdungs, Royal Coachman Wets and Black Gnats just to name a few. Bluegills loved them. And since most of my fishing at the time was a farm pond that was within a 5 minute walk away, I was living in my own little fly fishing utopia. But all the magazines would talk about top-water fishing. The "rise" was not something in my repertoire at that point of life. But I wanted it to be.

However, not being a fly tyer at the time and knowing no other fly fisherman who could help a young fisherman out, I had to take matters into my own hands. Literally. The next weekend of the summer found me shoveling horse and calving stalls at the local farm, tossing bales of hay down into the barnyard and schlepping milk cans from the stanchions to the bulk tanks. That following Monday found me on my bike, two miles down the road at the Black Crow bait shop and staring once more at the wall cards of Gaines poppers as usual. Only this visit I had come armed with hard earned cash. I was the only patron in the place at 10am on a Monday. The owner's wife had opened for me as was normal, since he didn't open himself on weekdays until after working his normal day job. She stood patiently at the register waiting for me to make my very difficult decision, with the sound of the minnow tank aerators the only sound in the small shop. It was tough. Although I knew nothing about anything I was looking at and there were so many danged colors! In the end, I went all out. Copying something I had seen in an article of Field–and-Stream magazine I chose a clear plastic 10 compartment box, and then put 2 of each of my 10 selections in in each compartment. I remember her looking at everything as I placed it on the counter. Her questionable eye was obvious. I had seen it before in my Mom at times of trouble which scared me a bit, but I held my ground stoically as she asked me if I wanted "all" of it. A firm nod and a "Yes ma'am" confirmed it. I was already holding out my hard-earned twenty dollar bill as she totaled things to $15 and looked up. She laughed at me as she took my money and asked, "Birthday or chores?"

"Neither" I replied, "I'm working at Dents Farm."

Her eyebrows lifted a tad bit and she smiled. "Good for you" she said and handed me my small bag of gear. I threw a "thank you" over my shoulder as I ran out the door. The sound of the screen door slamming on its spring was the last sound I heard before I was peddling down the gravel road. I was ready.

Within 10 minutes of arriving home everything was neatly aligned in the box and tucked safely in my shoulder creel. At the pond, things went surprisingly well. Casting had come fairly easy to that point now, so all I had to do was keep my poppers out of the weeds. With my very first cast things began to click. As I had read in the articles, you cast it out, wait for the rings to dissipate on the surface, and then give your popper a quick twitch. The cycle is repeated until your fly is either taken, or you reach the bank. Well, for the next 2 hours my little poppers never made it to the bank without at least a strike. The return trip home found me lugging a stringer of fat bluegills over my shoulder. I had experienced the "rise" and I was hooked from that point forward. Bluegill filets were my treat for dinner.

That moment in time occurred 41 summers ago. Yet it is a vividly clear memory for me, and I am thankful for that. Last weekend I took my youngest son who had just turned 11 to a local pond as well. He's still working on his casting, and though he had caught some fish on a fly they had all been with a nymph/indicator rig. We tied on a small deer hair popper that I now tie at my own bench and within moments he was smiling over a ten inch bass that had sucked in his offering. I had watched in anticipation as he listened to my instructions, and felt an involuntary flinch as the swirl appeared beneath his popper. It was as if I was willing him to set the hook. By the end of the evening he had landed a half dozen fish and he was securely hooked on fishing poppers. "These flies are so cool Dad" was his comment each time he would look into my fly box to change patterns. I could see the wonderment in his eyes as he tried to make a decision on which popper to choose next. "Let's use this yellow and black one".

"Yellow works Bud", I replied with a smile. And with that I was right back in the Black Crow bait shop staring up at those cardboard popper cards.

But for Memories

The Briar Creek that I grew up near was the epitome of a perfect wild brook trout stream. A fact that was not contemplated during my youth yet became painfully obvious as I traveled through adulthood. It was a true rarity. A jewel of the outdoors that not only was in its prime as I knew it, but was also mostly left alone by local fishermen. It was perfection within the trout world, and the best of trout streams to a 12 year old boy with a hand-me-down fly rod and a tin of wet flies. To that boy, it was water equal to any of those found in the pages of magazines, with brookies so brilliant and plentiful that no rival was possible. At least in my young mind it was so.

237

R.E. Long

The creek was formed by two forks. The East fork flowed from a spring near the base of Knob Mountain, and then travelled through farm fields and two beaver dams. From the point of the second beaver dam downstream to its confluence of the west branch it was intermittently brush choked with a few stretches of hemlock shrouded runs. This was an ecosystem of its own as the beaver dam was full of large fish, and the lower run was in essence a tail-water fishery. We would begin at the dam until we had caught a brace of keepers, and then move downstream, pool-hopping between us through the hemlock runs.

The west fork was fed from a spring that had long ago been formed into a farm pond. From that point its gradient increased rapidly and its pocket water tumbled down through a mile and a half of hemlocks, where it met with the east fork. This pocket water stretch taught me everything I needed to know about fly fishing so many of the waters I encountered later in life out west. I learned by trial and error how a drifting wet fly "needed" to be presented in order to even be looked at. Later I would come to realize that the fish on Briar Creek came to the creel with much more difficulty than most waters I had encountered since.

It was at the confluence of the two forks that a large pool formed in the shade of several old hemlocks, before gaining speed and heading out through meadows

One Small Trout

where it dumped into the local watershed. It was a beautiful place to behold. With just enough room for casting, small gravel bars to approach the water, and almost an ethereal feeling while in the shade of those huge dark trees. It was the genesis of this fisherman's piscatorial memories and the birthplace of so many pans of frying fish in my mom's kitchen. Quite often through the years I will find myself sitting along other waters yet daydreaming about that hemlock pool. More waters than I can count have taken me back there. It seems that my mind has decided that place "is" fishing. Not able to understand exactly why my mind works in that fashion, I've willingly accepted that fact and not fought it. After all, it did treat me well, so who am I to complain simply due to a lack of understanding?

A few years back I realized that I had not fished that water in many years. So with rod in hand I took the trip back home and made my way through the woods from that familiar gravel road. However, things had changed. There was no longer a watershed as I had known it. In an effort to fix a damaged and dangerous dam, the watershed had undergone a complete transformation. At the beginning of those old meadows the creek was now routed underground. The entire area of the confluence was now open grass. Gone was the pool. Gone were the hemlocks. Gone was all that I had known and loved for so many years. Not giving it enough time to sink in, I turned away and began fishing

my way back up the west fork and its pocket water.
Some fish were still there, but most were in the 5 inch
range. Still as beautiful as ever, but far fewer than I
recalled. I fished casually upstream for about ½ mile,
then turned around and strolled back down to the
location of the old pool. With a dozen fish on the walk I
still could not shake the sadness of what had become of
my pool. Sitting on a stump on the edge of the tree line
where the meadow began, I looked out over the old
location. It was gone, but I could still sense it. Closing
my eyes I could hear the streams currents converging. I
could smell the thick heavy air under the canopy of the
hemlocks, and feel the pea-gravel move under my high-
top converse sneakers. I was there. It was there. Just as I
had often found myself while sitting on the banks of
waters far better known and heralded. And it was then
that I understood. But for memories many things such
as this small stretch of water would at some point cease
to exist. Not just go away, but cease to exist as if it never
had existed at all. Unless it's existence and meaning was
held in the memories of those in which it had touched.

Furnace Green

If you like classic streamers, the Furnace Green needs to reside in your box. Inspired by a good friend of mine to design a signature Rangeley Style Streamer, it in turn has become a pleasure to fish, accounting for some of my largest fish across Pennsylvania's waters. Whenever a pattern that is so much fun to tie becomes so effective; you cannot help but share it. This one is mine.

Furnace Green Recipe

Hook: #6 Daiichi 2370 Dick Talleur

Thread: 8/0 Black Uni-thread

Rib: Medium Gold Tinsel

Body: Green Uni-floss

Under-wing: Olive Buck tail

Over-Wing: 4 Pheasant tail fibers

Throat: Red Buck tail

Wing: Opposing Furnace hackles

Shoulder: Hen pheasant shoulder feathers

One Small Trout

<u>Tying Instructions</u>

1- Tie in the tinsel about one eye-length behind the eye, and wrap back to a point even with the barb of the hook.

2- Bring the thread back to the tie-in point and tie in the floss, wrapping back to a point even with the point of the hook.

3- Form an even body with the floss toward the front of the hook, tying off at the original start point.

4- Wrap the tinsel forward up the shank to the rear of the floss, then palmer an even rib forward, tie off and add a small amount of head cement at the tie off point.

5- Tie in the red buck tail on the underside of the hook with the tips extending to the point of the hook.

6- Tie in a sparse bunch of olive buck tail on the top of the hook extending back to point 2 gap-lengths past the bend of the hook.

7- Tie in the pheasant tail fibers arching over the olive buck tail, extended to the same point.

8- Apply a small amount of head cement or superglue to the tie in point, whip finish.

Prepare the wing

9- Identify two opposing furnace hackles of a length that once the base of the quill is stripped of webbing will extend to the same point as the olive buck tail.

10- Identify 2 opposing hen pheasant shoulder feathers with the white center-line and evenly strip the quills clean.

11- Using a dab of super glue or head cement marry and attach each shoulder feather to the appropriate furnace hackle.

12- Once dry, mount each assembled wing/shoulder to the appropriate side of the hook.

13- Build a clean tapered head, whip finish and apply desired head cement.

Little Tan Caddis

The cold clear water of the Shenandoah Valley's Dry River enveloped my waders from the knees down as I eyed the riffle upstream of my position. There was no hatch or surface activity visible, but on this brook trout stream the lie I was after looked to be a good bet. The little 3 weight glass rod flexed well into the cork as I put 20 feet of double-taper line in the air, then dropped the little #16 Elk-Hair Caddis within inches of my target. The diminutive offering danced in the riffle for a mere 3 feet before it was taken in an aggressive roll accompanied by a small tail-slap as if to say "it's mine!" The take left me with the impression that it was not the only fish in the lie that was after my fly. The 8 inch fish fought like twice his size, a credit to its Char lineage, and I enjoyed the battle which was perfectly suited for the rod in hand. Easing it toward the gravel tail-out where I stood it came to hand calmly. The distinctive vermillion back shrouding haloed red and blue markings were beautiful in the spring sun as I popped the fly from the corner of its mouth and watched with satisfaction as it darted from my hand, lost again to the streams bottom. Brook trout always seem to make me smile.

A quick check of the fly for any possible damage, I rinsed it in the stream and pinched it dry before putting it back in the air to further dry with a few false casts. As I eased back into position to check on whether he had a few more of his kin hiding out in the riffle, I thought about the fly itself. Having had the fortune to fish across the country in the waters that trout call home, one thing has always remained a constant; each-and-every water carries a Caddis hatch. And to narrow it down even further, each-and-every water carries some form of a "Tan" caddis hatch. It may vary in size from the size 20 micro-caddis of Pennsylvania's Tulpehocken Creek, to the lumbering size10 tan-winged caddis on Washington States Olympic peninsula. But the one constant is, they can all be effectively fished with similar tan, down-winged caddis pattern with a body shade at least close to the streams naturals.

As a result, like many others I tend to default to a like pattern when first hitting a particular stream, whether it's familiar water or a first time visit.

One Small Trout

Whenever there is an absence of hatch activity but a desire to fish the surface, it is the most logical choice. Fish see caddis, and fish remember caddis. They have saved the day even when there has been an abundance of mayfly activity, but no willingness to rise and take anything in my box. Despite the present mayflies, they will step to the side and grab that Caddis pattern by reflex as it drifts overhead. An experience once again reinforced as my fly made it a scant foot before being slapped at once and then heartily taken on the second rise by a near mint version of the 1st fish. You just can't help but love the Caddis.

While any stream that holds caddis will also fish well with caddis larva and a myriad of bead-head patterns, my first choice are replicas of the diminutive moth-like critter as a dry fly. The traditional Elk-Hair Caddis or EHC has accounted for more fish than I can possibly count. It works. Very little else is needed to describe its merits. Add to that a plethora of existing patterns from the well-known CDC and Elk to the Fluttering Caddis, Tent-wing Caddis and simple CDC Caddis. They all catch fish by adequately imitating the little tan-winged caddis. My personal favorite these days on my eastern waters is the Penns Grannom. A turkey tail fiber bodied version of a CDC and Elk and a Fluttering Caddis. It does very well for me, and is most often the first pattern I tie on. It floats well, is durable and fish like it.

R.E. Long

There are times, as I stand rigging for a day on the water, that I find myself tying on a Caddis and stop myself. It almost feels like cheating. I "know" a caddis pattern will pull up fish. Maybe I should dig a little deeper into the well and try to crack the code-of-the-day for what the fish are truly feeding on. Many times I choose that route and find rising trout willing to take my example of the hatch they are eating, and other times will find me ending the day with a caddis pattern on my tippet. These days the other aspect of a little tan caddis pattern is that in low light it's easy to see which is a testament to aging eyes as much as anything else. It is simply far easier to track in riffles than a size-22 Blue-winged Olive pattern. I reckon it is what it is.

A few holes further down the stream I was watching as the sun began to dip below the treetops. An orange hue was cast across slow, shallow glide and the chirping birds were gone. It was that moment on a warm spring day, when the transition from birds and wildlife would soon be replaced by crickets and peepers. The brief period of relative silence that comes and goes without notice unless you are paying attention. Tonight it signaled that this would be my last pool. I waded out slowly, more for casting room than position. Not a dimple was on the surface. My line could be heard in the air as I worked out line, and as the fly lit on the water it formed a lonely singular ring on the surface. For a moment it did not seem to move in the

248

One Small Trout

slower flow of water. And then as if in no hurry, a head arose and opened showing a bright white mouth and a speckled dorsal fin porpoised in the location where my fly had been. A lift of the rod kicked things into motion with the thrashing of a large struggling fish as it stayed on the surface. A violent struggle in protest of the little tan caddis fly set firmly in the corner of a jaw.

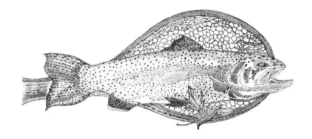

The 20 Incher

Ever since I can remember growing up along the limestone streams of Central Pennsylvania, my world and what was important involved trout. From the brook trout streams in and around my home, to the storied waters near State College and Carlisle where authors fawned over their merits and made us all wish to wet a line. In the beginning any fish was worthy. Yet we would read the articles and dreamt about one day casting a size 22 Blue-winged olive on one of those "other" waters, only to see it sipped in by a nose only slightly smaller than the front bumper of a VW Bug. It would take us into our backing and end with a beautifully shellacked mount on our cabin wall. A cabin that looked just like the ones we saw each Saturday morning on American Sportsman. It was so clear to me how it would be. All I had to do was get there.

Those days however were replaced with reality, and the soon acquired knowledge that a true trophy was better gauged by the waters one was fishing. A fat 10 inch native brookie on a stream narrow enough to jump over at any point was the trophy fish of bigger waters we saw on TV. And in the world of stocked public waters a holdover 16 inch fish is a trophy that takes every bit of fishing prowess any larger fish would require. Reality taught us that we were never going to see the 20-inch native brook trout of Canada's wilds in central Pennsylvania. It was another world. The 24 inch rainbows of Calgary's Bow River were just not part of our ecosystem. Neither were the beautiful 18 inch Yellowstone Cutthroat we saw in all the magazines. So although the waters around us would occasional surprise us with some extremely large hook-nosed browns, it was probably going to be the fish of a lifetime when-and-if it ever happened.

Be-what-may, eventually the dreams of mounting that big fish faded. I would see others mounted and think that it would be cool to have, but the driving force of early years just wasn't there anymore. To justify those changes in my own mind (as if there was something wrong with that mindset), I told myself that I would not mount anything unless it was 20 inches

One Small Trout

or larger, and caught on public water. Private water in my mind did not count, since water managed to produce large fish simply will. And I found them. But those 20 inch plus fish on private guided waters, though beautiful and amazing to catch, fell short of driving me to the taxidermist. Was I finding excuses to "not" mount a fish? Or simply setting the bar too high? Many years went by, including a dozen on the West Coast where steelhead and salmon entered my reality. Now what would I do? Is a 26 inch summer -run native steelhead a rainbow or not? Did it count? And once caught, what did that do to my vision of a 20 inch public water fish? Was it now somehow diluted? Either way, I moved along, with no mounted fish on my non-existent cabin wall. Until I found myself back east again and in my limestone waters of old. All thoughts at that point had faded of ever mounting a fish. I had completely removed it from my thought process.

Then one fall afternoon I found myself wading the upper pools of the Yellow Breeches; one of those storied trout waters I grew up reading about. I was working a pod of fish that were flashing in a small run and doing pretty well for the day. When the bite died down, I took a few steps downstream and decided to try dredging the deep pool below me. On the second cast the indicator dipped and I set the hook. It was big! Not being able to wade downstream through the deep hole I hung on for dear life and watched as the fish took me

253

nearly into my backing. Then, against all odds and my 6X tippet, I began working the fish back upstream. Two additional runs later and I was kneeling over a rainbow like I had not seen before. I gazed down at the tail that lapped over the 20 inch mark on my net and it hit me. I had done it! After about a minute's hesitation my mind resolved the situation and I moved to take care of the fish. A couple of pictures lying on the net and the fish was back in my hands and in the water. As the fish quickly revived my mind began to work. What should I do? I had set that goal more than 20 years earlier, and it would truly be a beautiful mount. My hands opened and the heavy pulse of its tail against my palm told me it was gone and my decision had been made. I gathered up my gear and moved to the bank, sitting with my feet still in the water. I was as content as a fisherman has a right to be at that very moment.

Today, I look up over the tying bench in my den and smile. In a frame is a picture of that fish, below it is a pencil sketch I completed shortly after releasing it. It's a memory of a perfect fish, on a perfect day, on water often dreamed about throughout my youth. It's about a goal set, and the understanding once achieved, that the only real value held was in my mind and in that very moment; a moment where the only requirement was a fly rod in hand and a fish willing to rise.

While Standing in Water

A year passes and another begins as the cycle repeats itself, leaving behind a mental fresco of waters. A painting in vivid display that rolls along through the walls and caverns of your mind reflecting many things in which you already knew would hold a place, yet many in which no significance was felt at the time. It's a painting of value which is permanently bonded with your memories. You cannot erase it. Nor could you truly affect its creation. Your part was in choosing to "be there" in those moments of time adjacent to the memory painted. By simply placing yourself in the path of the brush you affected each stroke, and each moment applied the pigment. Those colors are what carry through year-to-year for me. They are the continuity that, regardless of the final painting, all was as it should

255

be in the end. They lend a sense of understanding to my personal fresco.

My year always begins on the cold palate of a world in grey-scale, where nature adds it's occasional bright whites and soft Sepia's to make things "pop". All is subdued in my eyes. Even the movement and pace throughout the day become a color of the season. The grey hues paint the smoothness of birch in contrast to the course and gnarled black walnut. Distinct individually, but blending in a monochromatic nature that only winter can provide. Some fight it on their own grounds, wanting the color to return in its most pleasurable form. But I tend to embrace it for what it is. It's a time for care. Where a wading misstep cannot just make you recoil from the cold water, but affect your day in far more dramatic fashion. It's a time when even the silvers and champagne pinks of a rainbow's flanks provide the highlights to the shortened fights and willingness to come to hand.

As spring transitions into view green takes control. It is the exclamation point to the high waters and slightly too cold rain that carries with it the expectation of warmer days ahead. Fish take on the attributes of the weather, going from hot-to-cold just as quickly. A time of Spring Gobblers and the arrival of the year's first bugs, even though the conditions at times turn off the fish in the same breath, causing one to take pause in the seemingly wasteful nature of an otherwise wonderful hatch. But when the fish turn on, they do so with a certain gusto that only spring can spawn. They are hungry just as we are, and they respond in kind. For me this is a time for streamers, violent strikes and memories of my Dad, minnow bucket tight to his side and a fish on. Spring carries with it the many memories of traditional season openers and the artist takes a broad brush.

Summer, like winter, is a time to slow things down and pick your times. They are bright days and sudden thunderstorms bringing torrid and muddy waters. The heat takes its toll on both fish and fisherman alike, where a slower pace and a welcome sanctuary are keys. The long evenings mean heavy hatches in the fading light of dusk and frantic swallows soon to be followed by bats. Where you find one fish you will find them all, as the common need for cool waters draws them together. My summers are times of fiberglass rods, light tippet and stalking the dawn in search of wild brown trout before the first rays of sun touch the water. A perfect cast and a fish willing to rise to my dry fly presentation is what pulls the most vibrant colors of summer to view. It feeds me and makes the greys of winter stand in contrast even that much more. Those are days when I smell of bug juice, sweaty waders and fish, punctuated by a much appreciated cold beer during recovery.

R.E. Long

Fall is both the peak and a fitting end to the season, and nature has a way of closing things out with dramatic flair. Nothing in nature compares with the colors of fall, when even the fish take on the brilliant colors of their surroundings. The vermillion backs of native brook trout explode in contrast and the orange spots and buttery gold of brown trout are things to behold. Fish know when fall arrives, and they slash and chase as October brings the largest bugs of the year. The haunt of the deer woods pull me in separate directions through autumn, with each year declaring no clear winner. It's a time of my largest fish, warmest memories and a time for reflection. My approach changes and technical fishing is replaced by large caddis dries accompanied by tandem bead-heads. Both fisherman and fish scramble for the last vestiges of life before the leaves drop and the greys of an uncertain winter looms.

Each piece of a year on the water is a wonder unto itself, worthy of celebration on its own merits. But when brought together on a piscatorial palate, for those willing to place themselves in the way of the painter they form a work of art surpassing all value. Each year a new fresco appears in my mind. Each one different, yet all are special in their own ways. Included are children's smiles, special days, flies tied, remembered fish, water shared with friends and pieces of myself. A masterpiece, painted perfectly on the walls of my mind while standing in water.

GONE FISHING

R.E. Long

Previous books by the Author include

Tomorrow's Fish

The Telling of Waters

A Boy, His Bow and The First Season

Thrones of Granite

Made in the USA
San Bernardino, CA
28 April 2015